Safe to Fail

Also by Thomas F. Huertas

CITIBANK, 1812–1970 (*with Harold van Buren Cleveland*)
CRISIS: Cause, Containment and Cure
THE FINANCIAL SERVICES REVOLUTION (*co-edited with Catherine England*)

Safe to Fail

How Resolution Will Revolutionise Banking

Thomas F. Huertas

First published 2014 by
PALGRAVE MACMILLAN

Palgrave Macmillan in the UK is an imprint of Macmillan Publishers Limited, registered in England, company number 785998, of Houndmills, Basingstoke, Hampshire RG21 6XS.

Palgrave Macmillan in the US is a division of St Martin's Press LLC, 175 Fifth Avenue, New York, NY10010.

Palgrave Macmillan is the global academic imprint of the above companies and has companies and representatives throughout the world.

Palgrave® and Macmillan® are registered trademarks in the United States, the United Kingdom, Europe and other countries

ISBN: 978–1–137–38364–8

This book is printed on paper suitable for recycling and made from fully managed and sustained forest sources. Logging, pulping and manufacturing processes are expected to conform to the environmental regulations of the country of origin.

A catalogue record for this book is available from the British Library.

A catalog record for this book is available from the Library of Congress.

Contents

List of Illustrations   vi

Acknowledgements   viii

List of Abbreviations   ix

Introduction: Resolvability Will Determine the
Future of Banking   1

1   "Too Big to Fail" Is Too Costly to Continue   4

2   Less Likely to Fail: Strengthening Regulation   21

3   Less Likely to Fail: Sharper Supervision   50

4   Safe to Fail   82

5   Setting Up for Success   134

Conclusion: Is Basel Best?   173

Notes   178

Bibliography   193

Index   207

List of Illustrations

Boxes

1.1	Resolution determines risk to investors	16
2.1	Risk inside the ring fence: a look at the UK legislation	42
3.1	How re-hypothecation works	69
4.1	Resolution through sale to a third party: unlikely to be a tool for G-SIBs	93
4.2	A hybrid approach to resolution	129
5.1	Banks as intermediaries	145
5.2	What to do about loans	152
5.3	Scoring conduct risk	158
5.4	How an OpCo can improve efficiency	171

Figures

1.1	Crisis depresses global GDP	4
1.2	A $13 trillion cheque: official support to the financial system, 2007–2009	12
1.3	Prior stimulus has reduced fiscal flexibility	12
1.4	Implicit government support raises overall rating	18
2.1	Basel III raises capital requirements	22
2.2	Leverage ratio depends on lens used to measure assets	27
3.1	Distance to resolution drives supervisory classification	60
4.1	Resolution: tight time frames dictate advance planning	84
4.2	Bail-in via stay on investor capital	97
4.3	Coordination can create continuity	104
4.4	Resolvability hinges on structure of liabilities	113
4.5	A resolvable banking structure	114
4.6	Balance sheet overview	115
4.7	Bankruptcy of parent	117

4.8	Bank with foreign branch: resolution under unitary approach	118
4.9	Resolution under a territorial approach	120
4.10	Banking group with domestic and foreign subsidiaries	122
4.11	SPE approach requires concurrence of home and host	125
4.12	Structural subordination makes deposits significantly safer than parent company debt	133
5.1	Supervisory strategy to reduce risk	136
5.2	Regulatory reform requires strategic response	139
5.3	Banks need to set a sustainable target for risk and return	140
5.4	Creating shareholder value	141
5.5	An activity-based view of banking	144
5.6	Emerging economies drive growth in financial services	149
5.7	Calculating risk capacity	156
5.8	Setting a buffer between risk capacity and appetite	157

Tables

1.1	G-SIBs as of November 2013	7
1.2	G-SIBs account for the bulk of activity in key products	9
1.3	G-SIBs participate in multiple FMIs	10
1.4	Interdependence between banks and governments	17
2.1	Basel III hardens the definition of capital	23
2.2	High-quality liquid assets eligible for the LCR buffer	33
4.1	Resolution regimes: implementation of FSB key attributes	85

Acknowledgements

Although this book does not necessarily represent the views of Ernst & Young, I am deeply grateful to my partners and colleagues at the firm for discussion of the issues and for the opportunity to work with them to advise clients on how they might meet the challenges that the new regulatory environment will pose.

This book expands the arguments made in a number of articles and papers that I have written since joining Ernst & Young at the beginning of 2012, including "Safe to Fail" and "Getting Risk Governance Right," each of which was published in the *Journal of Financial Perspectives* and "A resolvable bank" which the London School of Economics Financial Markets Group published as a Special Paper. I am also grateful to discussants at seminars at the London School of Economics Financial Markets Group, at the Johann Wolfgang von Goethe University in Frankfurt and at the Bank of Spain.

Finally, and most importantly, I would like to thank my wife and my son for their continuous encouragement and support. Without them, the book would not have been possible.

List of Abbreviations

AML	Anti-money laundering
BCBS	Basel Committee on Banking Supervision
BIS	Bank for International Settlements
BoE	Bank of England
CCAR	Comprehensive capital analysis and review
CCP	Central counterparty
CET1	Common equity Tier 1 capital
CFO	Chief financial officer
CFP	Contingency Funding Plan
CFTC	Commodity Futures Trading Commission
CPSS	Committee on Payment and Settlement Systems
CRO	Chief risk officer
DTA	Deferred tax asset
ECB	European Central Bank
ESRB	European Systemic Risk Board
FATF	Financial Action Task Force
FBO	Foreign banking organization
FCA	Financial Conduct Authority (UK)
FMI	Financial market infrastructure
FPC	Financial Policy Committee (UK)
FRB	Board of Governors of the Federal Reserve System
FSB	Financial Stability Board
FSF	Financial Stability Forum
FSOC	Financial Stability Oversight Council
FTT	Financial Transaction Tax
G-20	Group of 20
GAAP	Generally accepted accounting principles
GLAC	Gone-concern loss absorbing capacity
G-SIB	Global systemically important bank
G-SIFI	Global systemically important financial institution
HMT	Her Majesty's Treasury (UK)

IA	Internal audit
IFRS	International Financial Reporting Standards
IIF	Institute of International Finance
IMF	International Monetary Fund
IOSCO	International Organisation of Securities Commissions
ISDA	International Swap Dealers Association
KYC	Know your customer
KYCC	Know your customer's customer
LCR	Liquidity coverage ratio
LGD	Loss given default
LIBOR	London interbank offered rate
LTI	Loan to income
LTV	Loan to value
MBS	Mortgage-backed securities
MPC	Monetary Policy Committee (UK)
NSFR	Net stable funding ratio
OpCo	Operating services subsidiary
OTC	Over the counter
PD	Probability of default
PRA	Prudential Regulation Authority
RAF	Risk Appetite Framework
RAS	Risk Appetite Statement
RoA	Return on assets
RoE	Return on equity
RWA	Risk weighted asset
SEC	Securities Exchange Commission (USA)
SME	Small- to medium-sized enterprise

Introduction: Resolvability Will Determine the Future of Banking

The future of banking depends on whether or not banks become resolvable, that is, whether they can fail in an orderly manner at no cost to the taxpayer and without significant disruption to financial markets or the economy at large. In other words, can banks become safe to fail?

Resolvability makes banks like other firms. If banks are resolvable, investors, not taxpayers, bear the cost of bank failures. Moreover, banks can continue in operation while in resolution, much the way airlines continue to fly even in bankruptcy. In other words, resolvability assures that banks can "die" in the market. This possibility should give banks greater scope to live in the market – to set their own strategy and make their own decisions.

In contrast, if banks cannot die in the market, it is unlikely that policymakers will permit banks to live in the market. If taxpayers rather than investors are to bear the cost of bank failures, banks will either become wards of the state, or they will be broken up. The former would diminish efficiency and hamper growth; the latter could well make the financial system more brittle, not less.

Much therefore rides on whether or not banks can become safe to fail, both for banks themselves and for the society at large. This book starts with a summary of what is at stake, why it is so important that we end "too big to fail" (Chapter 1). Briefly put, "too big to fail" is too costly to continue. It destroys the public finances. It distorts competition and removes market discipline. Worst of all, it encourages risk taking. If continued, it could possibly sow the seed for the next crisis. For all these reasons, we need to put an end to too big to fail. But we need to do so in a manner that preserves the contribution that finance can and should make to growth and development.

That involves two steps, each coordinated by international committees meeting in Basel in response to a mandate received from the G-20 heads of state. The first step is to make banks less likely to fail. This entails strengthening regulation (see Chapter 2) and sharpening supervision (see Chapter 3). The improvements in regulation are similar to the covenants that banks would impose on borrowers, and the increased intensity of supervision is similar to the efforts that banks would take to monitor and enforce those covenants.[1] If implemented globally, the improvements in regulation and supervision would indeed reduce the likelihood that banks could fail.

Basel III sets the international standard for stronger regulation. It raises capital requirements, introduces liquidity requirements and strengthens prudential standards. These measures increase the likelihood that the bank will remain in sound condition.

Less certain is the impact of various structural reforms, such as the separation of commercial and investment banking within a group and the imposition of various forms of ring fencing. These have not been agreed to in Basel, but created in an uncoordinated manner in different jurisdictions. Such reforms will certainly fragment financial markets and reduce efficiency. They will not necessarily improve the safety of individual institutions or the stability of the system as a whole.

Sharper supervision involves not only enforcing the tougher requirements, but also taking a more rigorous, more proactive and more forward-looking approach to supervision so that the supervisor can intervene in a timely manner to get the bank to take corrective action. This applies not only to prudential issues, but also to conduct ones. Although conduct supervision is increasingly separate from prudential supervision, the former has significant implications for the latter, as conduct violations have led to fines and restitution requirements large enough to have a significant adverse impact on the reputation and capital of the offending bank.

However, neither stronger regulation nor sharper supervision can make banks fail-safe. Nor should they attempt to do so. Indeed, if banks are to fulfil their function as intermediaries between issuers (borrowers) and investors (depositors), they must take risks. This implies that there remains a risk that banks will fail.

Chapter 4 outlines how banks can be made safe to fail, or resolvable, so that investors, not taxpayers, bear the cost of bank failures. Much of the groundwork has already been accomplished. The chapter fills in the details on what remains to be done, including how resolution can be implemented for globally active banking groups.

Resolvability will not only impact banks in death, it will affect them in life as well. Indeed, regulation and supervision will establish the framework in which banks must operate. This will pose a strategic challenge for banks, and Chapter 5 explains what banks need to do to meet that challenge – how they can set themselves up for success.

The book concludes on a positive note. The reforms to regulation and supervision will certainly make banks less likely to fail. Indeed, banks are already significantly stronger and likely to become stronger still. What is needed to make banks resolvable is also clear, and both the authorities and the banks are making significant progress toward that end.

But both authorities and banks need to take action to complete the job. That will make banks safe to fail as well as less likely to fail. This in turn will pose a strategic challenge for banks – one that they can either pass or fail as competitors in a global market. This is far superior, both for banks and society at large, to the fragmentation and regimentation that could result if banks are deemed to be unresolvable.

1

"Too Big to Fail" Is Too Costly to Continue

Finance is central to the growth and development of the world economy, and a relatively small number of global systemically important financial institutions (G-SIFIs) are central to finance. But this interdependency is dangerous. The failure of one or more G-SIFIs could disrupt financial markets and put the world economy into a tailspin. Even if such a decline could be arrested, it may take many years before output again reaches its pre-crisis level and many more before it attains levels consistent with the pre-crisis trend of growth rates. Thus, crises can be quite costly, particularly if they permanently scar the economy (see Figure 1.1).[1]

A case in point is the "Great Recession" – economist-speak for the sharp downturn and sluggish recovery that followed

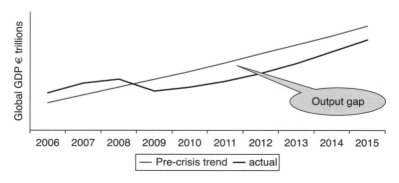

Figure 1.1   Crisis depresses global GDP

the bankruptcy of Lehmans in 2008.[2] In fact, the Great Recession is already one of the costliest crises on record. At the start of 2014, output remained well below what it would have been had growth continued at the pre-crisis trend rate and in some markets, notably the United Kingdom and most countries in the Eurozone, output remained below pre-crisis levels. Like a boxer who has struggled back to his feet after having been knocked down, the world economy is shaky. In such a situation, another financial crisis could deal the world economy a knock-out blow.

Should such a crisis recur, governments would be hard pressed to respond as they did in 2008, when they provided vast amounts of solvency and liquidity support to banks and other financial institutions. This support has, along with the recession itself, reduced the capability of governments to respond to a future crisis, should one develop.

So it makes sense to reform regulation and supervision, for doing so can reduce the likelihood and/or severity of any future financial crisis. However, financial intermediation requires financial institutions to assume risk if they are to contribute to growth and development. If financial institutions are to do their job properly, they cannot be failsafe. So it also makes sense for regulation and supervision to assure that finance can in fact take – in a controlled manner – the risks appropriate for an intermediary to assume.

In short, regulation and supervision have to strike a balance between stability and growth. The key to doing so is reforming resolution, so that failing financial firms can be reorganised and restructured without cost to the taxpayer and without significant disruption to financial markets or the economy at large. That will promote stability, for it would very significantly reduce the probability that the failure of one firm, however large and however complex, could trigger a financial crisis. And that in turn will allow regulation and supervision of banks and other financial institutions to focus on assuring that financial firms are taking and managing risk properly rather than forcing such firms to avoid risk entirely. In other words, if financial firms can be made safe to fail, they need not, indeed should not, be made failsafe.

Finance is central to growth and development

Finance makes two contributions to growth and development. It makes investment more productive, and it augments the amount of investment that takes place.

To see why this is the case, imagine a world without finance. Investment would be restricted to projects that a firm or family could afford to pay for out of their current resources. That would limit total investment and reduce its productivity. Many good projects with high risk-adjusted returns would simply not make it to the drawing board, much less off it.

In effect, finance allows issuers – the users of capital – to compete for the accumulated savings that investors have at their disposal. Hence, there is flow of capital to projects with higher risk-adjusted returns. This raises the yield on investment and makes saving more attractive, increasing the volume of saving and therefore investment.

The job of finance is to assure that this competition does in fact take place; that it is fair to both issuers and investors and that prospective returns are aligned with the risk to which the investor is exposed. To do its job of promoting growth and development, the financial system has perhaps above all to generate liquidity. It has to transform long-term illiquid assets (e.g., loans) into short-term liquid liabilities (e.g., deposits) and/or it has to allow investors to sell or buy assets without the mere act of their placing an order causing the price of the asset to fluctuate.

To achieve such a maturity transformation or to generate such market liquidity for investors, the financial services firm must itself assume a variety of risks – credit, interest-rate, exchange rate, counterparty, operational, and so on. It is the job of each financial firm to manage these risks. And it is the job of regulators and supervisors to

- ascertain that financial institutions exhibit good conduct and punish those who don't; and
- confirm that financial institutions remain in good condition (meet threshold conditions) and put into resolution those who don't.

It is not the job of regulators or supervisors to make banks failsafe. That can't be done, or at least it can't be done without undermining the very function – risk-taking – that makes banks socially useful.

Global systemically important banks are at the core of the financial system

At the heart of the financial system are the 29 banking groups designated as global systemically important banks (G-SIBs; see Table 1.1).[3] Collectively, they account for a very significant share, if not the bulk of the world's financial activity.

Table 1.1 G-SIBs as of November 2013

HQ jurisdiction	Supervisor	Bank	Surcharge (%)	Assets ($ bill)	Capital ($ bill)
USA	FRB	JP Morgan Chase	2.5	2,359	160
USA	FRB	Citigroup	2.0	1,864	136
USA	FRB	Bank of America	1.5	2,212	155
USA	FRB	Goldman Sachs	1.5	938	66
USA	FRB	Morgan Stanley	1.5	780	54
USA	FRB	State Street	1.0	222	13
USA	FRB	Wells Fargo	1.0	1.422	126
USA	FRB	Bank of New York Mellon	1.0	359	16
EU/EZ/Ger.	ECB	Deutsche Bank	2.0	2.654	66

Continued

Table 1.1 Continued

HQ jurisdiction	Supervisor	Bank	Surcharge (%)	Assets ($ bill)	Capital ($ bill)
EU/EZ/ France	ECB	BNP Paribas	2.0	2,516	99
EU/EZ/ France	ECB	Crédit Agricole	1.5	2,649	81
EU/EZ/ France	ECB	Group BPCE	1.0	1,513	61
EU/EZ/ France	ECB	Société Générale	1.0	1,649	50
EU/EZ/Italy	ECB	Unicredit	1.0	1,222	64
EU/EZ/Neth.	ECB	ING	1.0	1,102	52
EU/EZ/Spain	ECB	BBVA	1.0	841	46
EU/EZ/Spain	ECB	Santander	1.0	1,674	81
EU/NEZ/UK	BoE/PRA	HSBC	2.5	2,692	151
EU/NEZ/UK	BoE/PRA	Barclays	2.0	2,350	80
EU/NEZ/UK	BoE/PRA	RBS	1.5	2,069	88
EU/NEZ/UK	BoE/PRA	Standard Chartered	1.0	636	40
EU/NEZ/SE	SE FSA	Nordea	1.0	893	31
Switzerland	FINMA	Credit Suisse	1.5	1,007	47
Switzerland	FINMA	UBS	1.5	1,373	44
Japan	J FSA	Mitsubishi UFJ	1.5	2,709	129
Japan	J FSA	Sumitomo Mitsui	1.0	1,718	78
Japan	J FSA	Mizuho	1.0	2,049	74
China	CBRC	Bank of China	1.0	2,015	121
China	CBRC	ICBC	1.0	2,788	160
Total				48,292	2,383
Total as % of top 1000				43%	39%

Notes: EZ = Eurozone; NEZ = non Eurozone.
Source: FSB (2013b) and The Banker database.

Without reform of resolution, the failure of any one of these institutions could have severe repercussions on financial markets and on the world economy.

Of the 29 G-SIBs 16 are headquartered in Europe, 8 in the United States, 3 in Japan and 2 in China. Supervision of G-SIBs will fall predominantly to two institutions: the ECB (after banking union becomes effective, it will directly supervise 9 G-SIBs) and the US Federal Reserve System (8). The Bank of England's Prudential Regulatory Authority will also play a significant role, as the home supervisor of the 4 G-SIBs headquartered in the United Kingdom and as the host-country supervisor for the activities of the other 25 G-SIBs in the world's primary international financial centre.

Collectively, the G-SIBs account for approximately 40 per cent of the total Tier 1 capital and total assets in the global banking system (see Table 1.1). They also account for the dominant share of activity in key financial markets (see Table 1.2). In payments, nine out of the top ten banks in international cash management services are G-SIBs. Collectively, G-SIBs have over $100 trillion of assets under custody, over 65 per cent of the total assets under custody. Eight of the top ten custodians are G-SIBs. In foreign exchange, G-SIBs account for over 90 per cent of FX trading, and each of the top ten players in the FX market is a G-SIB. In loan syndication, bond underwriting and equity underwriting the story is similar. G-SIBs account for over 70 per cent of total volume and at least nine of the top ten players in each market is a G-SIB. In addition, each G-SIB is generally a leading player in the domestic retail market. Many G-SIBs have millions of retail customers (with the largest having a customer base of over 100 million individuals).

Table 1.2 G-SIBs account for the bulk of activity in key products

Product/market	Share of 29 G-SIBs in total (%)	# of G-SIBs in top 10 in the market
Payments	n.a	9
Custody	65	8
FX	90	10
Derivatives	80	10
Loan syndication	70	9
Bond underwriting	70	10
Equity underwriting	70	9

G-SIBs are also the principal participants in financial market infrastructures (FMIs), such as payment systems, trade settlement systems (e.g., for foreign exchange, loans and securities) and central counterparties (CCPs) (see Table 1.3). Hence, the failure of a G-SIB could put several

Table 1.3   G-SIBs participate in multiple FMIs

G-SIBs including subsidiaries	CCPs (11)	SSS (6)	PS (5)	Total (22)
Bank of America	8	6	5	19
Barclays	10	6	5	21
BNP Paribas	11	6	3	20
Citigroup	11	6	4	21
HSBC	9	6	5	20
JP Morgan Chase	9	6	4	19
Royal Bank of Scotland	10	6	5	21
Société Générale	7	6	4	17
UBS	11	6	4	21
Bank of New York Mellon	7	5	4	16
Credit Suisse	11	6	3	20
Goldman Sachs	11	6	1	18
Mizuho FG	6	5	4	15
Morgan Stanley	10	6	2	18
Deutsche Bank	9	6	5	20
Crédit Agricole	6	6	4	16
Mitsubishi UFJ FG	6	6	4	16
State Street	6	6	5	17
Wells Fargo	5	5	3	13
BBVA	3	6	3	12
ING	4	6	2	12
Standard Chartered	3	5	5	13
Bank of China	0	6	3	9
Santander	3	5	3	11
Sumitomo Mitsui FG	1	3	3	7
Unicredit Group	4	5	3	12
Nordea	3	5	3	11
Group BPCE	0	0	1	1

Note: CCPs (central counterparties): CME, ICE Clear Credit, OCC, NSCC, FICC, LCH Clearnet, ICE Clear Europe, CME clear Europe, NYSE Liffe, Eurex, Euro CCP; SSS (securities settlement system): Euroclear Bank, Clearstream Luxemburg, Euroclear UK and Ireland, Euroclear France, Clearstream Frankfurt; PS (payment system): CHIPS, CHAPS, TARGET 2, CLS, SWIFT.

Source: EY based on FMI websites.

FMIs under pressure at the same time. This could pose a significant threat to financial stability, for FMIs are "single points of failure." If the failure of one G-SIB causes an FMI to fail, this could topple over other G-SIB participants in the FMI. This could in turn cause disruptions in financial markets and in the economy at large.[4]

Containing the current crisis has exhausted the capability of governments to respond to another crisis

That economists speak of "The Great Recession" rather than "The Great(er) Depression" is eloquent testimony to the success of the policy measures that policymakers took in 2008 and 2009.[5] But these measures have reduced fiscal flexibility and largely exhausted the range of options open to monetary policy. Were another financial crisis to occur, governments would find it difficult if not impossible to respond as they did in 2008 and 2009.

Support for financial institutions contained the crisis

During the crisis governments provided massive amounts of support to their banking systems. This prevented contagion and limited the number and severity of failures. Either directly or in conjunction with central banks, governments injected equity into financial firms, guaranteed firms' borrowing in capital markets, increased deposit guarantees, provided credit to firms and supported, via massive acquisition programs, the price of asset-backed securities. Total direct assistance to the financial sector amounted to over 80 per cent of GDP in the United Kingdom and to nearly 75 per cent of GDP in the United States (see Figure 1.2).

But fiscal flexibility has evaporated

As a result of the support given to financial institutions as well as the recession spawned by the crisis, government debt relative to GDP has soared over the past five years (see Figure 1.3).

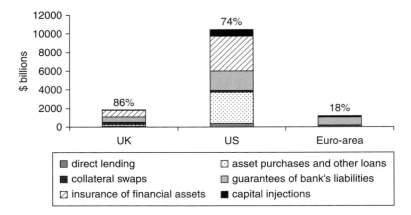

Figure 1.2 A $13 trillion cheque: official support to the financial system, 2007–2009

Note: Figure in per cent above the column represents total support relative to GDP.

Source: Bank of England, financial Stability Report, June 2009.

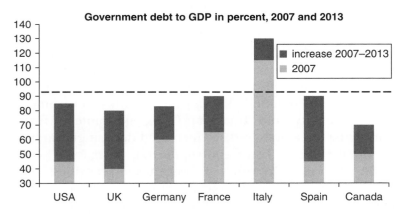

Figure 1.3 Prior stimulus has reduced fiscal flexibility
Source: IMF.

Indeed, in many jurisdictions debt levels have reached the point where a prudent finance minister must be concerned about the readiness of investors to continue buying his or her country's sovereign debt. The recovery remains weak, and in some quarters there is concern that we may be entering a period of "secular stagnation."[6] The possibility that a government would have to support its banks if they were to encounter difficulty only adds to investors' concern about the health of sovereign borrowers.[7] Indeed, some observers go so far as to characterise the link between sovereigns and banks as a "doom loop."[8]

And monetary policy is running out of options

Central banks today do not have the same degree of freedom that they had in 2008 and 2009. They have used much, if not entirely all, of the policy ammunition they had at their disposal to fight (and subdue) the crisis. They have little or no dry powder left.

Take interest rates as an example. When the crisis broke, rates stood at 2 per cent in the United States and at over 4 per cent in the Eurozone and in the United Kingdom. There was ample scope to reduce rates to stabilise and stimulate the economy. Today there is not. For all practical purposes central banks have reduced short-term interest rates to zero. Moreover, under a program known as "forward guidance" central banks have already stated that they will keep short-term rates at zero until unemployment recedes to pre-crisis levels.[9] Accordingly, there is not much more that a central bank could do on the short-term interest rate front. Short-term rates cannot fall much further and the promise to keep rates low already stretches as far as investors' eyes can readily see.

Central banks have also already created additional monetary stimulus through supplemental measures. In the United States and the United Kingdom this has taken the form of quantitative easing, the direct purchase of massive amounts of bonds by the central bank.[10] By concentrating their purchases on bonds in longer maturities, policymakers hoped to suppress long-term rates and so spur investment.

Additionally in the United States policymakers used quantitative easing to give support to the housing market: the Federal Reserve has purchased nearly $1.5 trillion in mortgage-backed securities.[11] This has contributed to suppressing the level of mortgage rates and ultimately to a revival in housing starts.

In the Eurozone the ECB has engaged in what might be termed "qualitative easing." During the course of the crisis the ECB relaxed the criteria for collateral that banks had to pledge against such loans, indicating that it would accept collateral of lower quality (credit rating) and collateral packaged into so-called own-issuance of asset-backed securities. Over the same period, the ECB offered banks unlimited access to term (three-year) liquidity. Together, these steps have vastly expanded the ECB's liquidity provision to the banking system.[12]

In sum, although these fiscal and monetary policy measures have contained the crisis, they have not as yet assured recovery. Should another crisis develop, it is not immediately apparent that policymakers have ample fiscal or monetary tools in reserve that they could use to combat it. Practically everything has been deployed to fight this crisis. If a new crisis were to develop, the authorities would have few, if any, additional measures in reserve.[13]

Ending too big to fail has top priority

That makes it all the more important to reduce the probability that a new crisis could develop. To this end the G-20 heads of state mandated the Financial Stability Board to identify sources of systemic risk to the world economy and to develop mitigation strategies against these risks.[14] Members of the G-20 formed similar bodies in their respective jurisdictions, including the Financial Stability Oversight Council (FSOC) in the United States, the European Systemic Risk Board in the EU and the Financial Policy Committee in the United Kingdom.[15]

These groups have all identified G-SIFIs as a systemic risk. Should one fail, it could cause significant disruption to financial markets and the economy at large. Although governments could potentially avoid such costs by providing taxpayer support to the failed institution, they have little scope to do so and every reason to assure that investors, not taxpayers, bear such costs.

Indeed, the prospect that governments would bail out the creditors of a G-SIFI is the very root of the problem known as "too big to fail." If investors expect that the government will rescue a G-SIFI rather than resolve it (and impose losses on the creditor), the market will judge the credit of the G-SIFI primarily on the basis of the credit of the government that would provide the backstop rather than on the likelihood that the G-SIFI would fail at some point to meet threshold conditions.

Too big to fail destroys the public finances

The prospect that governments could provide assistance on such a massive scale poses the threat that investors will simply transfer their poor regard of a G-SIFI to the government in which the G-SIFI is headquartered. If a government backs its banks, the government's credit will suffer as the condition of its banks deteriorates.[16]

Indeed, in the peripheral Eurozone countries, governments are hostage to the health of the banks in their jurisdiction. Should they have to rescue the banks, fiscal deficits would soar and the credit of the government would deteriorate – Ireland is Exhibit A for this. But banks are also hostage to the health of governments. Should governments default or reschedule, banks that had invested heavily in government debt could fail and require resolution and/or recapitalisation – here Greece is Exhibit B. Breaking this doom loop is one of the primary motivations for banking union in the Eurozone.[17]

Too big to fail distorts competition

If the market expects the government to bail out banks when they fail to meet threshold requirements for minimum capital and/or liquidity, then such banks can borrow at lower cost (see Box 1.1). This gives them an undue competitive advantage relative to institutions that are not likely to be bailed out.

Box 1.1 Resolution determines risk to investors

The resolution regime has a significant impact on the loss that investors expect when they extend unsecured credit to a bank and therefore on the risk premium that a bank will have to pay when it borrows.

	Too big to fail	Safe to fail
Probability that bank will fail to meet threshold conditions	20%	20%
Probability of rescue	95%	5%
Probability of resolution	5%	95%
Loss given resolution	25%	25%
Expected loss	25 bp	475 bp

A simple example illustrates why. Take an institution that is too big to fail. The probability that it will fail to meet threshold conditions and that intervention will be required is 20%. If the market judges that the bank is too big to fail, it is effectively stating there is a very high probability (say 95%) that the government will rescue the bank (so that there is no loss to investors). Correspondingly, the market is stating that there is a low probability (5%) that the authorities will place the bank into resolution. If the bank does go into resolution, the expected loss to investors is 25% of their exposure at the point of resolution. Accordingly, the expected loss to investors in the too big to fail bank is 25 basis points (bp).

Now make the same bank safe to fail. Assume there is no change in the probability that the bank will fail to meet threshold conditions (this remains at 20%). Assume as well that the loss the investor suffers if the bank does go into resolution remains at 25%. The only change refers to the probability that the bank will be rescued. If the bank is safe to fail this falls to 5% and the probability that the bank will be put into resolution rises to 95%. As a result, the expected loss to investors in the safe to fail bank is 475 bp.

Note that the probability of rescue is itself the product of two factors: the ability of the government to do so, and the willingness of the government to do so. Even if a weak government is willing to support its banks, it may not be able to do so (see Table 1.4).

Too big to fail removes market discipline and encourages risk-taking

Ordinarily, as a firm's risk of default rises, so does the risk premium that the firm is required to pay on its debt – a fact which may also reduce the firm's capacity to raise debt. Together, the increase in the risk premium and the reduction in the firm's debt capacity constitute market discipline.

But in the case of banks, market discipline may not work effectively. The risk to the investor in bank debt depends heavily on the likelihood that the government would bail out the creditor, should the bank need to be resolved (see Box 1.1). Debt providers will therefore look as much to the willingness

Impact on bank's overall creditrating of implied sovereign support

		Bank's stand-alone condition			
			Weak		Strong
Government's credit condition	Weak	◯	Impact limited as government is too weak to be a source of strength	◯	Impact zero and possibly negative as bank is stronger credit than the sovereign
	Strong	⬆	Impact positive as strong government can prop up weak bank	◯	Impact limited as bank already has strong credit rating.

Table 1.4   Interdependence between banks and governments

and ability of the government to provide support to the bank as they will to the strength of the bank itself (see Table 1.4).

If a weak bank is headquartered in a jurisdiction with a strong government, investors will factor the possibility that the government could support the bank and/or its creditors if the bank entered or came close to resolution. Indeed, the rating agencies have formalised this criterion. In rating a bank, they provide two ratings: the stand-alone rating without implicit government support, and the overall rating, which provides an assessment of the risk that the creditor will actually experience a loss. Generally, the overall rating is one or more notches above the stand-alone rating, with the difference between the two being a measure of the degree of support that the rating agency expects the government to give the credit, should the bank fail to meet threshold conditions and require resolution (see Figure 1.4).[18]

In effect, too big to fail aligns the credit standing of banks within a jurisdiction with that of the government that could provide the backstop to the bank's liabilities. Weak banks headquartered in jurisdictions with highly rated governments may therefore be able to raise funds at lower cost than would be the case if they had to raise funds purely on the basis of their stand-alone credit rating. This differential is

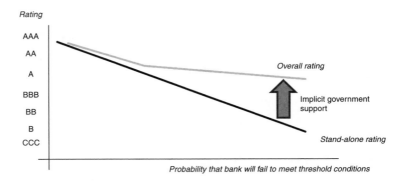

Figure 1.4   Implicit government support raises overall rating

effectively a subsidy to banks, especially to those with weak stand-alone ratings.[19]

In sum, if the market expects the government to bail out a G-SIB, the market will not necessarily discipline the bank. This will encourage risk-taking at the bank and may make the bank more likely to fail. Thus, bailing out G-SIBs could well be sowing the seeds of the next crisis – a crisis that may be all the more severe, given the exhausted state of government finances and the importance of G-SIBs to finance (see earlier).

The reform agenda is well on the way to completion

Avoiding such a scenario has been one of the main drivers for wide-ranging reforms to regulation and supervision of banks in particular and finance in general. Briefly put, these reforms aim to do two things:

1. *To make banks less likely to fail.* This entails stronger regulation (see Chapter 2) and sharper supervision (see Chapter 3). These reforms are already in place, and banks have already taken steps to strengthen their capital and improve their liquidity.
2. *To make banks "safe to fail,"* so that they become resolvable at no cost to the taxpayer and without significant disruption to financial markets or the economy at large. Banks and the authorities have made considerable progress towards the most important regulatory priority and arguably the "litmus by which the public judges the success of the entire reform programme".[20] Major jurisdictions have introduced effective resolution regimes in line with the key attributes identified by the Financial Stability Board. G-SIBs have developed resolution plans, and resolution authorities are in the process of developing cooperation agreements. Although some issues remain, making banks resolvable is a task that is on its way to completion (see Chapter 4).

These regulatory reforms will reshape finance, for they broadly determine the risks firms may accept, the capital firms must keep, the liquidity firms must maintain, the conduct firms must observe, the governance firms must use and the risk to which a firm's creditors will be exposed, if the firm fails. In other words, regulation and supervision set the boundaries within which a firm may choose its strategy (see Chapter 5).

These boundaries will be much tighter than those prevailing before the crisis. As a consequence firms will have to reset their return targets, reshape their business models and constrain their risk appetite to fit within their risk capacity. To earn their cost of capital, firms will have to concentrate on businesses where they have a competitive advantage, streamline costs, sharpen controls and refine risk management.

In other words, banks will face the prospect that they can die in the market. No one will bail them out. But in return banks will get the opportunity to live in the market. That is far preferable to the alternative. If banks do not become "resolvable" (so that they can fail without cost to the taxpayer and without significant disruption to financial markets or the economy as a whole), pressure will build up to make them much simpler as well as to make them much, much smaller, even though this could adversely affect growth and development. In other words, if banks cannot die in the market, they may not be permitted to live in it.

2

Less Likely to Fail: Strengthening Regulation

To make banks less likely to fail, authorities in all principal jurisdictions have decided to strengthen regulation. Using the agreements in the Basel Committee on Banking Supervision as a foundation, authorities have raised capital requirements, instituted liquidity requirements and set standards for governance, risk management and remuneration. Together these measures will reduce the likelihood that banks will fail.

Less certain is the impact of various measures, such as structural reform, that individual jurisdictions such as the United States and the United Kingdom have implemented. As these measures are not coordinated internationally, they will lead to fragmentation of financial markets and reduce efficiency, without necessarily reducing risk or improving resolvability.

Increasing capital requirements

Capital that is immediately available to absorb loss – tangible common equity – serves as the primary bulwark against failure. This is just as true for banks as it is for non-financial firms. Banks that have a greater loss-absorbing capacity are less likely to fail. In the crisis the prevailing capital regimes proved insufficient to absorb the losses that banks incurred – despite the fact that banks maintained capital significantly in excess of the minimum requirements in force at the time.

Consequently, reforming capital requirements has constituted the first plank of the reform program. This has four aspects: (i) hardening the definition of capital, (ii) increasing capital requirements, (iii) tightening the rules determining the calculation of risk-weighted assets and (iv) introducing a leverage regime as a complement to the risk-weighted regime. Together, this means a vast increase in capital requirements (see Figure 2.1).

Basel III hardens the definition of capital

First of all, and perhaps most significantly, the basis for bank capital requirements has shifted towards a tangible common equity standard, or capital that is unequivocally and immediately available to absorb loss whilst the bank remains a going concern. This new standard, called common equity Tier 1 (CET1) capital, is a much tougher standard than the core Tier 1 capital standard that had prevailed under Basel II as it excludes certain items that had previously qualified as core Tier 1 capital (see Figure 2.1). Moreover, practically all

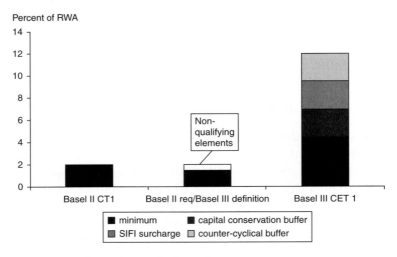

Figure 2.1   Basel III raises capital requirements

bank capital requirements are now expressed in terms of the tougher CET1 standard.

To harden the definition of capital, the Basel Committee eliminated or limited the ability of banks to count towards the new CET1 standard anything other than tangible common equity (see Table 2.1).[1] Tangible common equity counted under Basel II and continues to count under Basel III. However, goodwill no longer counts at all under Basel III – such assets cannot be readily turned into cash and such assets are particularly prone to write-offs, if the bank fails to realise the synergies that led it to bid a premium for the acquired company.

Basel III also placed limits on the ability of a bank to count other items towards CET1 capital.[2] Under Basel II, deferred tax assets, mortgage servicing rights and investments in the capital instruments of other financial institutions were all included in core Tier 1 capital. Under Basel III, these assets are in principle deductible from CET1 capital. However, as a compromise the members agreed to put the aggregate of deductions under these categories into a so-called sin bucket and to restrict the deduction from CET1 capital to the amount in the sin bucket that exceeded a threshold equal to 15 per cent of the bank's CET1 capital.[3]

	Basel II Core Tier 1	Basel III Common equity Tier 1
Tangible common equity	●	●
Goodwill	●	○
Deferred tax assets	●	"sin bucket"
Mortgage servicing rights	●	◑
Investments in other financial institutions	●	

Table 2.1 Basel III hardens the definition of capital

Basel III raises capital requirements

In addition to hardening the definition of capital, Basel III significantly increases capital requirements. The minimum equity capital requirement will rise from 2 per cent of risk-weighted assets (RWAs) in "old money" (core Tier 1 capital) to 4.5 per cent of RWAs in "new money" (CET1 capital). In addition, banks will become subject to a capital conservation buffer of 2.5 per cent and the largest, most complex banks, the G-SIBs, will be subject to a surcharge (addition to the capital conservation buffer) of up to 2.5 per cent of RWAs (see Table 1.1). Finally, banks could become subject to an additional counter-cyclical capital requirement of up to 2.5 per cent of RWAs (see Figure 2.1).

Strictly speaking, the capital conservation buffer does not constitute a minimum capital requirement.[4] Instead, it represents the level at which the bank has to conserve capital by limiting dividends and distributions and by limiting bonus payments in cash to management and employees – ample reason in the eyes of many analysts and market commentators to regard 7 per cent as the effective minimum requirement. Should a bank fall below the 7 per cent capital level, it has to file a plan with its supervisor as to how it will restore its capital to that level. Until the bank's CET1 capital falls below 4.5 per cent, there is no requirement that the bank be put into resolution (although the supervisor may do so, if it judges that the bank has reached the point of non-viability for other reasons such as a lack of liquidity and an inability to finance itself in private markets).

The systemic surcharge applies to G-SIBs (see Table 1.1) and expands the capital conservation buffer applicable to that bank.[5] For a G-SIB with a surcharge of 2 per cent of RWAs, the capital conservation regime (limitation on dividends and distributions, etc.) would kick in when the bank's common equity Tier 1 capital fell below 9 per cent of RWAs.

The counter-cyclical buffer also expands the capital conservation buffer.[6] This is a macro-prudential tool (see later) that gives the authorities the ability to increase capital requirements on exposures to borrowers in a specific jurisdiction, if the authorities come to the conclusion that the economy as a whole or a specific sector is overheating.

Basel III tightens the risk-weighted regime

In addition to hardening the definition of capital and raising the required ratio of capital-to-risk-weighted assets, the Basel Committee also tightened the risk-weighted regime. It has increased requirements (i) on the trading book, particularly with respect to positions involving equity-like tranches in securitisation issues,[7] and (ii) for counter-party risk.[8] In addition, the Committee conducted a fundamental review of the trading book[9] – this may portend further tightening as would a possible requirement that banks use the standardised approach as a backstop or floor for the model-based approach.

Finally, the Basel Committee has started to assure that members implement capital requirements in a comparable manner so that the same asset would have roughly the same risk weight regardless of the jurisdiction of the bank that holds the asset.[10] Although most of the differences in risk-weighted assets relative to total assets stem from differences in portfolio composition or from differences mandated by supervisors or permitted under national derogations, some do stem from differences in assumptions that banks have made with respect to their models, particularly with respect to the probability of default and loss given default in low-risk portfolios (e.g., sovereign bonds). The Basel Committee has recommended that members take steps to remove differences introduced by the banks themselves. This would lead to a harmonisation of risk weights, ideally (at least in the eyes of the Basel Committee) by levelling up to the end of the spectrum with the higher risk weighting.

Basel Committee introduces a leverage regime

As a final element in the reform of the going-concern capital regime, the Basel Committee introduced a leverage standard as a supplement to the risk weighted regime.[11] Together the two ratios constitute what might be called a belt-and-braces approach to capital, each controlling different risks. The risk-weighted ratio controls overall risk, whilst the leverage ratio controls against overall balance sheet expansion as well as the risk that the models underlying the risk-based approach might be incorrect.[12]

The leverage ratio compares two numbers – capital in the numerator to assets in the denominator. So in concept leverage is simple: the ratio places a limit on the amount of assets that a bank can finance with debt. The higher the ratio (or the more the bank finances itself with equity), the lower the risk of the bank (all other things being equal).

It's when one starts to look at what's in the ratio that things get more complex. What counts as capital for the purposes of the leverage ratio? Total capital, Tier 1 capital, common equity Tier 1 capital before/after deductions of goodwill, deferred tax assets and other items in the so-called sin bucket? There are proponents and rationales for each of these definitions, but both supervisors and market participants appear to have converged on total Tier 1 capital as the standard to be used in calculating the numerator in the leverage ratio. This is a somewhat broader definition of capital than the CET1 standard underlying the risk-weighted regime and includes elements such as preferred stock as well as common equity.[13]

However, when it comes to assets, there is no common definition. The US measures assets using US GAAP. Most if not all of the rest of the world uses IFRS. The principal differences are the treatment of derivatives (GAAP uses the net figure; IFRS the gross or notional amount) and the scope of consolidation (GAAP allows certain assets to remain off balance sheet; IFRS generally brings such assets onto the balance sheet). So assets are higher under IFRS than under GAAP. That means the US leverage ratio (common equity to US GAAP assets) is higher than the "rest of world" leverage ratio (common equity to IFRS assets) would be (see Figure 2.2).

To put assets on a common basis that everyone could use, the Basel Committee took a third measure of assets, a regulatory definition of assets.[14] This strikes an effective balance between a ratio based on US GAAP and one based on IFRS and avoids appearing to require banks to adopt a uniform accounting standard. The Basel approach values derivatives at the net amount plus the amount that the bank would have to pay, if it needed to replace the contracts subject to netting (the replacement value) plus an amount to take into account the possibility that the bank's counterparties may be unable to perform (counter-party valuation adjustment [CVA]). This gives a value for assets that is somewhat higher than the value according to US GAAP but is significantly lower than the figure under IFRS. Accordingly, the same bank with the same assets will show a low leverage ratio under IFRS and a high ratio under US GAAP with the ratio according to the Basel definition lying between the two. In the example used in Figure 2.2, one and the same bank has a leverage ratio of 2 per cent under IFRS, 6 per cent under US GAAP and 3 per cent according to Basel. Consequently, stating that the banks should have a leverage ratio of 3 per cent will be a very strict standard, if assets are measured according to IFRS, still quite strict if measured under the Basel standard and not so

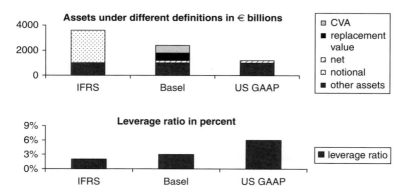

Figure 2.2 Leverage ratio depends on lens used to measure assets

strict if measured according to US GAAP.[15] Indeed, the crisis exposed the flaws in a leverage regime in place based on US GAAP. The US regime had only a limited effect, for US GAAP allowed banks to keep various entities, such as structured investment vehicles, off balance sheet and outside the leverage ratio.

Regarding calibration, Basel has proposed a minimum requirement of 3 per cent of exposure according to its definition to become effective in 2018. Banks have to calculate and report the ratio to supervisors from 2013 and they will have to disclose the ratio to investors and the public starting in 2015. However, once banks start to disclose investors will put pressure on the banks to meet the ratio as soon as possible.

In jurisdictions where distrust in the risk-weighted regime is strongest, supervisors have opted to implement a version of the leverage ratio early, so that this complements the risk-weighted regime more quickly. For example, in the United Kingdom the Prudential Regulatory Authority has, following a recommendation from the Financial Policy Committee (FPC), mandated that major UK banks meet the leverage requirement from 1 January 2014, a full four years earlier than the Basel proposal would require.[16] In addition, the Chancellor of the Exchequer has publicly requested the Bank of England to conduct a review of the leverage ratio and reminded the Bank that the PRA has the power to vary (increase) the ratio, should it consider it necessary to do so.[17]

In the United States the authorities have proposed that systemically important banks meet a tougher standard than that proposed by the Basel Committee. In addition to the minimum standard of 3 per cent under Basel III (and to the standard US requirement based on US GAAP) the United States proposes to introduce a buffer, similar to the capital conservation buffer, with respect to the leverage ratio. In order to qualify as "well capitalised" (and so have freedom to pay dividends and make distributions) systemically important US banks must maintain from 1 January 2018 a "Basel

III" leverage ratio in excess of 5 per cent at the consolidated holding company level and in excess of 6 per cent at the level of the subsidiary bank (insured depository institution). This constitutes a buffer of 2 per cent of total Basel III exposure over the minimum requirements established under the Dodd-Frank Act.[18]

Basel III increases loss absorbency of other forms of capital

Finally, Basel III took steps to improve the quality of Additional Tier 1 and Tier 2 capital. Specifically, the accord mandated that instruments such as preferred stock and subordinated debt could respectively continue to count as Additional Tier 1 or Tier 2 capital, if and only if they were subject to conversion (into CET 1 capital) or write-down when the bank reached the point of non-viability. Such conversion or write-down bails in the investors in such instruments and facilitates the ability of the supervisor and/or resolution authority to recapitalise a bank that is about to breach or has breached threshold conditions. This would promote resolvability (see Chapter 4) and the authorities are considering whether banks should be subject to a separate "gone concern" capital requirement that could be met by Additional Tier 1 and Tier 2 capital and possibly by other instruments subject to conversion or write-down at the point of non-viability.[19]

Introducing liquidity regulation

Liquidity is the lifeblood of banks, and lack of liquidity was the proximate cause of failure for many banks during the crisis. Although the Basel Committee had established general principles for sound liquidity management, there was no global standard for liquidity regulation until Basel III introduced one at the end of 2010.[20]

The new liquidity standard supplements the principles and promises to put bank funding on a much sounder footing. It has three parts. First, banks will be required to measure the liquidity risks that they run. This is the first step toward assuring that they can manage such risks. Second, banks will be required to hold a buffer of liquid assets sufficient to meet the net short-term (one-month) outflows of funds that the bank might experience under stress. Third, banks will be required to fund themselves in a stable manner. Taken together with improvements in liquidity supervision (see Chapter 3) the new liquidity standard promises to reduce significantly the liquidity risks that banks may run and correspondingly reduce the probability that lack of liquidity could cause the bank to fail.

Measuring liquidity risks

The first, and possibly most important, step toward assuring that banks have adequate liquidity is the requirement that banks (i) measure the liquidity risks that they run, and (ii) estimate the cash they could raise, if stress were to materialise. After all, what gets measured generally gets managed.

The measurement starts with establishing the outflows of funds that a bank is contractually obligated to make and the inflows of funds that it is contractually expected to receive (e.g., from the interest and amortisation payments that borrowers make on the bank's outstanding loans). Such a contractual schedule also needs to include contingent contracts, such as back-up lines of credit or pre-payment options, where the outflow or inflow depends on the condition of the borrower, the state of a market and/or the level of a macro-economic variable, such as the rate of interest.

The bank then has to adjust this contractual schedule to take into account funding concentrations (by provider, by product and by currency) as well as the behaviour of both lenders to the bank (including depositors) and borrowers from the bank. Such behaviour will depend not only on general economic conditions, but on the condition of the borrower and on the condition of the bank itself. To be on the safe side, liquidity regulation demands that banks use a stress scenario to make such behavioural adjustments to the contractual schedule of outflows and inflows. The stress scenario should envisage a combination of bank-specific and market-wide shocks that constrict some or all funding inflows into the bank whilst simultaneously accelerating funding outflows. The end result is an estimate of the net cash outflows that the bank might experience under stress over a 30-day horizon.

Banks also need to estimate the resources that they would have available to meet net cash outflows. This requires the bank to establish what might be called a collateral budget. This tracks – in current market value terms – the amount of unencumbered assets available to the bank, and estimates the amount, timing and location of the cash the bank could realise, if it were to sell the asset or use the asset as collateral to raise funds from private lenders and/or central bank under one or more of its normal lending facilities. Such a collateral budget should take into account the potential additional demands that counterparties will place on the bank to post collateral as the condition of the bank deteriorates as well as the possibility that lenders of collateral to the bank will run on the bank, just as lenders of cash (e.g., uninsured depositors) are withdrawing their funds. In particular, the bank should evaluate the probability that clients would curtail or cancel the ability of the bank to re-hypothecate to its lenders the securities that the client had pledged to the bank.

Establishing a liquidity buffer

The second element of liquidity regulation is the liquidity coverage ratio, a requirement that the bank maintain a buffer of unencumbered high-quality liquid assets sufficient to cover 100 per cent of the cumulative net outflow of funds that the bank might experience under the stress scenario outlined earlier. Ideally (and from the standpoint of sound liquidity management), assets in the buffer should be readily saleable in very large volumes at little or no reduction in price with immediate or same day settlement. Alternatively, banks should readily be able to pledge assets in the buffer as collateral to private lenders who are willing to give a high advance rate against the market value of the asset.

The trouble is that there are few, if any, assets that meet these ideal standards for market liquidity at all times. The nearest approximation to an ideal asset (from the standpoint of market liquidity) is a continuously and heavily traded government security issued by a sovereign in its own currency that is settled same day in central bank money (so that the selling bank can use the proceeds immediately to meet maturing obligations). However, most assets trade in relatively small quantities on a daily basis relative to the total stock outstanding. Nor is settlement necessarily immediate or even on the same day. So it is difficult to find assets whose sale can generate immediate cash without the bank incurring a loss and a further reduction in its capital.

For this reason, liquidity regulation sets out two categories of assets that are eligible to count toward the liquidity buffer (see Table 2.2). The first contains cash deposits at the central bank and liquid, frequently traded sovereign obligations with a zero risk-weighting under Basel rules. These assets are counted without limit toward the buffer at their full current market value (i.e., without a haircut). The second category of assets includes sovereign guaranteed obligations, high-grade corporate bonds and highly rated covered bonds from third-party issuers. This class is judged to be somewhat higher risk and/or to have greater price volatility. Correspondingly, such assets are subject to a 15 per cent haircut before counting towards the buffer, and there is a limit of 40 per cent on the aggregate amount of such Level 2 assets that the buffer may contain. In addition, the liquidity regulation gives countries the discretion to add a further sub-category within the overall Level 2 limit. This can account for up to 15 per cent of the total buffer and may include highly rated residential mortgage-backed securities (with 25 per cent haircut to current

Table 2.2   High-quality liquid assets eligible for the LCR buffer

Level	Description	Risk weight (%)	Rating	Price volatility	Haircut (%)	Maximum contribution to buffer
1	Deposits at central bank	0		Zero	0	100%
	Sovereign obligations	0		Low	0	100%
2	Sovereign guaranteed	20		Medium	15	
	Corporate debt		AA–	Medium	15	40%
	Covered bonds		AA–	Medium	15	
3	RMBS		AA–	High		15% of total, or 37.5% of Level 2
	Corporate debt		BBB– to A+	High		
	Corporate equities		n.a.	Very high		

Source: BCBS (2013b). RMBS = residential mortgage-backed securities.

market value) as well as less highly rated (but still investment grade) corporate debt securities and corporate equities (each subject to 50 per cent haircut from current market value).

Finally and perhaps most importantly, it should be stressed that the liquidity buffer is there to be used, if stress materialises.[21] Falling below the LCR does not push the bank into resolution – rather it is a sign that the bank is undergoing stress (or mismanagement) and a prompt for it to take corrective action, such as initiating its contingency funding and/or recovery plans.

Assuring stable funding

Finally, liquidity regulation also aims to assure that banks fund themselves in a stable manner. To this end Basel III developed the concept of a net stable funding ratio (NSFR).[22] This effectively sets a limit on the degree to which the bank can fund long-term assets with short-term liabilities so that the bank can withstand an extended (one year) idiosyncratic stress such as a decline in profitability, a credit downgrade and/or an attack (justified or not) on its reputation. However, the NSFR is not as well developed as the LCR and is likely to undergo further refinement/revision prior to its introduction as a formal requirement (currently proposed for 1 January 2018).

The stable funding ratio estimates the portion of each asset class that should be supported by stable funds. The longer the maturity and the less liquid (saleable) the asset is, the greater is the requirement for stable funding. Taken together, the estimates for each asset class yield a requirement for stable funds for the bank as a whole.

This requirement can be met by liabilities that

1. do not require repayment at all (e.g., Tier 1 capital, including common equity and perpetual debt/preferred stock);
2. require repayment at a distant maturity (e.g., debt with a remaining maturity of more than one year); or
3. have a short-term contractual maturity, but can be reasonably expected to roll over, even in a stress scenario (e.g., insured retail deposits).

Conversely put, the net stable funding ratio limits the reliance that a bank can place on funding sources (e.g., short-term unsecured wholesale funding) that are likely to run, if the bank starts to get into trouble and/or markets begin to dry up.

Risk governance

In addition to setting quantitative standards for capital and liquidity that banks must meet, regulators are also providing guidance as to how banks should govern the assumption and control of risk. If implemented well, this too should reduce the risk that banks will reach the point of non-viability.

Establishing a risk appetite framework

Good risk governance starts with a requirement that banks establish a risk appetite framework (RAF).[23] This should set the basis on which the bank takes risk to implement its strategy and accomplish its business objectives. The RAF therefore constitutes the bank's overall approach to risk-taking, and includes "policies, processes, controls, and systems through which risk appetite is established, communicated, and monitored." The RAF should take both a top-down and bottom-up perspective, and it should assure that the two are consistent with and reinforce each other. And, the RAF should apply, not only at the overall group level, but also at each of the group's principal legal vehicles.

Banks then need to write risk appetite statements (RAS) that articulate their risk appetite frameworks in a way that enables the business to implement the framework. The RAS should provide a top-down perspective. It should state "the aggregate level and types of risk that a firm is willing to accept in order to achieve its business objectives." The RAS should cover all risks, including hard-to-quantify risks such as operational and business conduct risk and combine quantitative measures, such as the impact that risk-taking could have on earnings, capital and liquidity, as well as qualitative measures such as the impact that risk-taking could have on the bank's reputation.

Above all, the RAS should ensure that the bank's risk appetite fits within its risk capacity, where risk capacity is defined as "the maximum level of risk the firm can assume before breaching constraints determined by regulatory capital and liquidity needs and its obligations, also from a conduct perspective, to depositors, policyholders, other customers, and shareholders." Risk appetite is "the aggregate level and types of risk a firm is willing to assume within its risk capacity to achieve its strategic objectives and business plan."

Risk limits embody the bottom-up perspective. They "allocate the firm's aggregate risk appetite ... to business lines, legal entities, specific risk categories, concentrations, and as appropriate, other levels." In aggregate, the composite provided by the collection of risk limits should mesh with the top-down statement of risk appetite.

According to the Financial Stability Board, the bank's board of directors should assure that the bank has a sound RAF – yet further evidence of the increasing responsibility for good governance that supervisors are demanding that boards assume. Management should be responsible for the development of the RAF. The CEO (with the support of the CFO and CRO) should set the tone from the top, so that the RAF and RAS influence the risks the bank decides to take or not take and how the bank manages the risks it does take. In short, the CEO should see that the RAF and RAS are embedded in the culture and operations of the firm. In particular, the CEO should see that risk appetite remains within risk capacity. The actual development of the RAF and RAS, including setting risk limits and monitoring adherence to risk appetite, should fall largely to the CFO and the CRO. Internal audit should verify that the RAF is in place and working as it should. The FSB emphasis on management's roles with respect to a bank's RAF is part and parcel of the greater supervisory emphasis on individual responsibility and accountability (see Chapter 3).

Strengthening risk data

To implement a risk appetite framework effectively, a bank must have comprehensive, accurate and timely data on risk exposures. This is essential if the bank is to be able to control exposures relative to limits or establish sensitivity to changes in risk factors such as interest rates, economic conditions or the credit-worthiness of particular counterparties.

Accordingly the Basel Committee has issued guidelines that call upon banks to strengthen their processes with respect to the acquisition, maintenance and analysis of risk data.[24] The objective is to make a bank's risk data as accurate as its accounting data; to make the risk data available in a timely fashion; and to improve the bank's ability to analyse the data. This starts with establishing data integrity. A taxonomy has to be established so that each counter-party has a unique legal entity identifier and that each exposure is linked to the underlying factors that determine the risk of the asset (e.g., the data on a mortgage exposure should also be linked to an estimate of the value of the house that serves as collateral for the loan). The risk data should be automatically updated as transactions occur. This will not only facilitate monitoring adherence to limits, but also give an accurate and up-to-date starting point for the analysis of risk and the development of mitigation strategies. Indeed, such capability is critical in a crisis – otherwise the bank will be operating behind a blindfold.

Remuneration

Regulating the incentives that banks can provide to management and staff is the final principal element in the global reform program. The main objective is to assure that remuneration is consistent with effective risk management.[25]

Prior to the crisis it was not. Bonus could be paid immediately in cash based almost entirely on the revenues that the particular business unit had achieved. In an environment where management had the ability to front-load revenues from long-dated transactions and/or an ability to secure intra-bank funding from other divisions at below market cost, the bonus arrangements induced greater risk-taking, particularly in trading businesses.

Remuneration reform puts a stop to these practices and puts remuneration on a much sounder footing. Bonus award determination cannot be based solely on revenues, but must take risk into account, including the prospective recipient's record with respect to compliance and audit issues. Bonus cannot be paid entirely in cash, but must include a performance-related element (such as stock or subordinated debt) so that the recipient is likely to suffer, if the bank's overall condition deteriorates. Nor can the recipient immediately obtain the entire amount of bonus that s/he has been awarded. A significant portion of the bonus award must be deferred and subject to claw-back, if subsequent events (e.g., compliance violations) reveal flaws in the original basis for determining the recipient's bonus award. Together these changes should largely assure that remuneration is in line with effective risk management.

However, many jurisdictions have started to regulate the amount as well as the form of compensation that can be paid. For example, the EU has limited bonus to 100 per cent of base salary (200 percent, if shareholders approve). The effectiveness of such a bonus limit is open to question. First, it has raised fixed costs rather than reduced average compensation, for banks have responded to the bonus limit by raising base salaries and introducing fixed allowances. This in turn has lowered the portion of total compensation subject to deferral and claw-back, diminishing the effectiveness of such measures in controlling risk. However, the limit has been effective in capping possible rewards for success. This provides employees who consider themselves likely to exceed the norm with an incentive to migrate to firms that are not subject to the cap.

Outside Basel

For various jurisdictions, notably the United States and the United Kingdom, the Basel program was too little, too late and/or too lax. These jurisdictions therefore supplemented the Basel program with measures of their own to reform bank structure and tax bank balance sheets and/or banks' activities. Ostensibly, the measures are intended to reduce risk and/or improve resolvability. They do not necessarily do so, but they will fragment financial markets and reduce efficiency.

Bank structure: is separation sensible?

In many jurisdictions authorities have proposed and in some cases implemented measures to insulate banks from "risky" trading activities. This insulation takes various forms – pushing derivatives out into a separate subsidiary, ring-fencing the commercial bank or the trading activities or simply prohibiting proprietary trading. However, these measures have three drawbacks. First, they are not coordinated with one another. Indeed, in some cases they contradict one another. As a result, they will fragment financial markets. That will certainly reduce efficiency. Second, separation measures are based on a false premise: that trading activity is inherently riskier than "traditional" banking activity, such as commercial loans. That is certainly not the case. Commercial banking can be every bit as risky as investment banking, and poorly run commercial banks are almost certainly riskier than well-run investment banks. So separation alone will not reduce risk. Nor will separation necessarily enhance resolvability. Third, separation may prevent the commercial bank from responding to the innovation and evolution that could take place in financial services in the future. If such ring-fenced banks cannot adapt to the future, they may become candidates for the cemetery.

Derivatives market reform and swaps push out

Derivatives played a prominent role in the crisis. They helped magnify the losses from sub-prime, for they allowed participants with no direct loan exposure to sub-prime to take a position on sub-prime. Derivatives were also opaque. As there was no central repository of trade information, it was difficult for either market participants or regulators to observe or control the aggregate amount of contracts that any one party had written and the degree to which the market as a whole had a concentration risk on a particular counterparty. As the failure of AIG demonstrated, this could have adverse effects on the system as a whole. Finally, derivatives carried considerable operational risk: participants had allowed considerable confirmation backlogs to build up. They had also failed to prevent the practice of unauthorised assignments from spreading.

To control these risks regulators combined steps at the micro or institution-specific level to strengthen the counter-party risk regime (see "Basel III tightens the risk-weighted regime" earlier) and improve data management and disclosure (see "Strengthening risk data" earlier) with measures at the macro level to improve the workings of the market as a whole. These macro measures include a requirement (i) that all OTC derivative contracts be reported to trade repositories and (ii) that standardised contracts trade on exchanges or electronic trading platforms and be cleared through central counterparties (CCPs). To reinforce the incentive of banks to implement these macro measures, Basel III included provisions to accord counter-party exposures to CCPs a lower risk weight. Any bilateral OTC derivative exposures that remained would be subject to higher capital and margining requirements.[26]

Although this reform holds significant promise (reduced risk of a financial crisis),[27] it also poses significant risks to the financial system. The first risk is a concentration risk: pushing transactions into CCPs is risk-reducing, if and only if the CCPs are each robust. If the CCP is not, then central clearing will compound, not reduce systemic risk. If the failure of a participant were to cause the CCP to fail, this could bring the market to a halt and cause other participants to fail. For this reason it is vital to assure FMIs in general and CCPs in particular be robust (i.e., able to withstand the simultaneous failure of their two largest participants) (see "Assure financial market infrastructures are robust" Chapter 3).

The second and much more immediate risk is fragmentation. Different jurisdictions have implemented the general principles differently and a number of jurisdictions, notably the United States, are attempting to apply their regime in an extra-territorial manner. Although authorities have attempted to reconcile the different approaches and even agreed (in the case of the United States and EU) on a so-called Path Forward there remains a threat that what has been a global market will fragment into a series of national markets with conflicting documentation and eligibility requirements.[28] Indeed, the US insistence that foreign CCPs and foreign banks comply with US rules regarding trades with US persons makes fragmentation almost a certainty, unless other jurisdictions are willing to harmonise their rules to those adopted in the United States.[29] Such fragmentation would reduce the liquidity of the market and raise costs to issuers, investors and other end users.

Further fragmentation could result from the implementation of the so-called Swaps Push Out rule in the United States, a provision included in the Dodd-Frank Act over the objections of the bank regulatory and supervisory agencies. The rule would require banking groups to "push out" their derivative activities from the insured depository institution (bank), as this entity is alleged to receive government "assistance" in the form of deposit insurance and access to the Federal Reserve discount window. The rule is applicable to US banks and potentially to foreign banks with branches in the United States and will begin to bite upon expiration of the extended transition period that the supervisors have granted to banks.[30]

Separating investment and commercial banking

Separation of investment and commercial banking has long had considerable attraction for legislators, largely on the basis that the former is risky or speculative, whilst the latter supports the real economy so that keeping the two separate will promote the stability of commercial banks and the economy at large.

The United States has long required banks to separate commercial and investment banking. Even after the repeal of the Glass Steagall Act in 1999, the US banking groups had to conduct the underwriting and distribution of corporate securities (such as bonds and equities) within a separately capitalised non-bank subsidiary that is a daughter of a parent holding company and sister affiliate to the group's insured depository institution (commercial bank). However, this set up has not brought financial stability to the United States. In the crisis, stand-alone investment banks failed, single purpose commercial banks failed and diversified financial holding companies failed. There is no conclusive evidence to suggest that the separation of investment and commercial banking limits risk, fosters safety or enhances stability.

However, largely on the premise that separation has exactly those effects, the United Kingdom has introduced a requirement that banking groups take insured deposits in a separately capitalised bank with a separate board of directors ring-fenced from the rest of the group via restrictions on inter-affiliate transactions and limitations or outright prohibitions on conducting trading activities, transacting in derivatives or opening foreign branches (see Box 2.1). As a result, the ring-fenced bank would become very largely a purely domestic bank dedicated to "traditional" but essential banking activities, such as making loans and taking deposits.[31]

Box 2.1   Risk inside the ring fence: a look at the UK legislation

The risk of the assets in the ring-fenced bank (predominantly loans) is not fundamentally lower than the risk of assets excluded from the ring-fenced bank (e.g., corporate bonds in a trading account). Indeed, as far as the lender's claim on the borrower's cash flow is concerned, a senior unsecured claim structured as a loan ranks pari passu with a senior unsecured claim structured as a bond. The credit risk is the same. Restricting the bank from holding the bond and inducing the bank to hold the loan does nothing to reduce the risk that the borrower will default. Indeed, such a restriction may actually increase the risk to the bank, as the bond is generally more liquid than the loan.

Nor does the ring fence necessarily make the ring-fenced bank easier to resolve. The limit on derivative activity within the ring-fenced bank reduces but does not eliminate this barrier to resolution (see Chapter 4), but the fundamental reason why the ring-fenced bank may be easier to resolve is the priority accorded to insured deposits, not the prohibition on trading activity. The priority granted to insured deposits makes it theoretically possible to resolve the ring-fenced bank by cherry-picking the best of the bank's unencumbered assets, matching them against the insured deposits and transferring the combined asset-liability package, either to a bridge bank or to a third party. This is similar to the option that domestic depositor preference gives to the US authorities in resolving a US insured depository institution.

What makes the ring-fenced bank safer is higher capital. Under the UK legislation, the ring-fenced bank must meet higher capital requirements than the investment bank or the group as a whole on a consolidated basis. It is this higher capital requirement, not the composition of the bank's assets or the activities in which the bank may engage, that reduces the probability that the ring-fenced bank will fail to meet threshold conditions and be forced into resolution. However, in the course of resolution reform such higher requirements may be imposed on the group as a whole as well as on the investment bank in the form of minimum requirements for "gone concern capital" (again see Chapter 4). If so, the rationale for separation would diminish greatly and perhaps disappear entirely.

The EU is also considering whether to create a ring fence. Unlike the United Kingdom, however, the EU ring fence – if it is erected – will go around the group's trading activities rather than its commercial bank. According to Erkki Liikanen, the chair of the group of experts whose report will form the basis for the EU proposal, the key principle is that insured deposits should not be used to finance proprietary trading and other "high-risk" trading activities.[32] France and Germany have already erected barriers along these lines. Again, it is doubtful that such separation will make either the group as a whole or the commercial bank safer. The banking subsidiary has the scope to take as much or more risk as the investment bank affiliate – one need only recall that commercial real estate lending has been the source of countless bank failures and it is precisely such lending in which the commercial bank may continue to engage. If the commercial bank is safer than the investment bank, it is not because commercial banking is safer than investment banking. It is because the commercial bank is required to hold higher capital (see Box 2.1).

Prohibition on proprietary trading (Volcker Rule)

In the United States the Dodd-Frank Act requires banking groups to take separation one step further, that is, to stop proprietary trading altogether. The so-called Volcker Rule will become effective in 2015 and will prohibit banking groups from trading certain financial instruments as principal for their own account in the trading book and from making investments as principal in private funds, such as hedge funds.[33] However, the rule allows banks to engage in such activities if they are customer related or serve to hedge the risks in the commercial bank, so that the bank may continue to conduct market-making activities, hedge the risks in the commercial bank, make investments in securities in connection with liquidity management and sponsor private funds in connection with providing services to fiduciary accounts.

The rule does not apply to certain financial instruments, even though they may be traded. Such exempt instruments include securities issued by the US government, US agencies and US municipalities, even though all such securities have considerable price risk due to interest rate and/or credit (in the case of agencies and municipalities). Exempt instruments also include loans, even though loans are increasingly traded. Finally, the rule provides US banking groups with some scope to conduct proprietary trading activities in foreign markets.[34]

As this brief summary illustrates, the Volcker Rule is a very complex regulation that will require firms to establish and maintain extensive records as well as conduct a comprehensive and continuous compliance program. This will certainly be costly, and there is a distinct possibility that such costs may outweigh the benefits from the rule.

Subsidiarisation

In addition to separating investment banking from commercial banking, there is a growing trend toward requiring banks to conduct their activities (particularly where these relate to consumers and especially where insured deposits are involved) via subsidiaries rather than as a single bank with branches. This is leading to the balkanisation of the global banking system.[35] If taken too far, this will depress efficiency and impede development.

The rationale for subsidiarisation is simple. If governments are to support banks, they wish to restrict that support to the elements of the bank that they judge to be essential to domestic financial stability and/or to the welfare of people who vote in national elections. These elements are, above all, consumer deposits, loans to SMEs and the integrity of the payments system. Banks' activities in capital markets as well as those in foreign markets have little appeal to voters – indeed voters and therefore legislators have rebelled against the idea that taxpayers should again support the global operations of global banks.

The clearest expression of this sentiment comes from the UK Treasury. In its White Paper introducing the banking reform bill in the United Kingdom, it explicitly restricted its commitment to assure continuity to the UK ring-fenced bank and stated that the rest of the banking group could and should be resolved according to normal bankruptcy proceedings.[36] The Swiss government made a similar indication in introducing its structural reform, including a requirement that Swiss banking organisations be able to place their domestic Swiss operations into a domestic Swiss subsidiary that could be resolved separately from the rest of the group.[37]

These steps have prompted a response from the United States. The US authorities noted that the United Kingdom and Switzerland no longer stood behind the global operations of their respective banking organisations.[38] Consequently, the United States took the view that it would have to look after the US operations of foreign banking organisations (FBOs). If that was to be the case, the US authorities reasoned that the US operations of FBOs should meet within the United States the same standards with respect to capital, liquidity, governance and data management as US banking organisations. To facilitate this outcome (and assure that it would be the primary supervisor of FBOs in the United States) the Federal Reserve has mandated that FBOs form an intermediate holding company to hold all of the FBOs' US subsidiaries. This intermediate holding company would be a bank holding company subject to US rules, including stress testing (CCAR) and the US leverage requirements.[39]

The US requirement for an intermediate holding company is likely to prompt significant changes in bank structure, particularly in Europe (see Chapter 5). It may also prompt retaliation by the EU and other jurisdictions, so that US banking organisations would have to conduct their operations in the EU through a separately capitalised intermediate holding company or bank headquartered in an EU Member State.[40]

Taxing the banks

Taxation has always been seen as a tool to channel activity into the direction that policymakers desire. It is, of course, also a way to raise revenue and finance general expenditure. At times, the former may serve as a blind for the latter, especially as the incidence of the tax may fall, not on the entity on whom the tax is levied, but on those with whom that entity deals, in the form of increased prices or charges to customers, lower prices paid to suppliers and/or a contraction in the activity subject to the tax.[41]

Financial transactions taxes

Such is almost certainly the case with financial transaction taxes (FTT).[42] These are taxes levied on each transaction, either as a percentage of the value of the transaction or as a flat rate. If the rate of tax does not depend on the period for which the asset is held, the FTT will fall most heavily on assets held for very short periods.

This may depress such short-term trading activity (a result that proponents of FTT welcome) or divert it to markets and/ or participants not subject to the FTT (a result that proponents of FTT deplore). If FTT has either of these two effects, it will raise little in the way of revenue. Although FTT legislation contains anti-avoidance and extra-territorial provisions to limit diversion, the facts suggest that FTT can be successful for globally traded products such as foreign exchange and derivatives, if and only if the FTT is a global tax. However, the FTT can be successful (as measured by the revenues it raises) if the product is local and must be traded or settled in a single place. Equities are an example, and stamp taxes on share transfers/transactions regularly raise significant amounts of revenue for finance ministries (the UK stamp tax on equities is a prominent case in point).

In the wake of the crisis the European Commission proposed a wide-ranging global FTT on financial transactions, including derivatives. However, the United States opposed this on a global basis, and the United Kingdom objected to an FTT solely on an EU basis, so that the FTT initiative is likely to remain a collection of national taxes (although a number of EU Member States may combine in a coalition of the willing to create an FTT common to the signatories of a special agreement).[43]

Bank levies

Bank levies are a tax on the aggregate balance sheet of the bank. The theoretical case for the tax is twofold. First, large banks have received and may require taxpayer support, as they are too big to fail. The tax is a way for them to "pay" for such support. Second, reliance on wholesale funding, particularly short-term wholesale funding, poses significant liquidity risk to the bank in question and the system as a whole. A tax on such funding would reduce such reliance and promote financial stability.[44]

In practice, governments have imposed the levies on balance sheets above a certain threshold. The levies usually allow a deduction for insured deposits, and some reduce the rate for long-term liabilities. The levies usually take the form of an excise tax – and finance ministers have periodically raised the rate, much the way they put an extra penny on a pack of cigarettes or an extra penny on a pint of beer. The levy is generally not deductible from income tax, and there has been little attempt to coordinate bank levies with income tax across countries (with the result that banks may be subject to double taxation). Nor is there any indication that finance ministries contemplate reducing or eliminating the bank levy as banks become more resolvable (see Chapter 4) and the need for taxpayer solvency support recedes. At most, consideration may be given to earmarking the proceeds of the bank levy to build up a resolution fund (see later).

Resolution funds

Resolution regimes usually contain provision for a resolution fund, whose purpose is to absorb costs of resolution that cannot be assigned to investors. This is a levy on the industry, rather than taxpayers generally, and may be imposed either ex ante or ex post. If it is an ex ante levy, the question arises as to whether the resolution levy will be in addition to the bank levy or whether the proceeds of the bank levy will be earmarked to build up the resolution fund.

Summary

In sum, stronger regulation will go a long way towards making banks less likely to fail. In particular, the Basel program (higher capital requirements, a global liquidity standard, better risk governance and reform of remuneration) will reduce risk, especially if coupled with sharper supervision (see Chapter 3).

3

Less Likely to Fail: Sharper Supervision

Stronger regulation is not the only reason banks will become less likely to fail. Sharper supervision will play a role as well, both at the level of the individual firm and at the system as a whole. With respect to micro-prudential (individual firm) supervision, the authorities have become more forward-looking and more pro-active, making judgements on firms' business models and strategies and on firms' ability to execute their chosen strategy successfully. The authorities have also introduced a new concept, macro-prudential (economy-wide) supervision. Here, the authorities aim to analyse the system as whole, asssess the risks to financial stability and devise measures to mitigate these risks, including the risks that may arise from non-bank financial institutions and from shadow banking. Together, these supervisory measures reinforce regulatory reform and should make banks less likely to fail.

Micro-prudential supervision

As the crisis evolved, supervisors increasingly took a more forward-looking, pro-active stance toward supervision. This approach has become the new standard for micro-supervision. The aim is to keep the bank well away from the point of non-viability, but to prepare for the possibility that it might reach such a point.[1]

The micro-supervision program is quite comprehensive. It starts with assuring that the bank has directors and management who are fit and proper and that such individuals exercise good governance. The supervisory program continues with classification of banks according to their distance from the point of non-viability. To make such a judgement, supervisors are evaluating the bank's business model, its strategy and its management's ability to execute that strategy appropriately. Stress tests supplement this classification. They determine how the bank would fare under materially more adverse economic conditions. If the bank was either currently or prospectively in the danger zone (close to reaching the point of non-viability), the supervisor would induce the bank to take steps to strengthen its condition as well as prepare for the possibility that the bank would require resolution.

Assuring directors and management are fit and proper

Good governance starts with people who exercise good judgement. Assuring that banks have such persons in place as directors and executives is a necessary precondition for establishing an effective board of directors and responsible management.

For this reason regulation generally requires that directors and executives of banks be "fit and proper." "Fit" means that the person has the expertise and experience necessary to fulfil her or his duties as director and/or executive. In brief, is s/he likely to see the right thing for the bank to do? "Proper" is a character test: does the prospective director and/or executive have the integrity and fortitude to stand up for what s/he believes is right for the bank to do and the talent to bring others around to her or his point of view?

Sharper supervision starts with more intensive and extensive pre-screening of the candidates for directors and executives at banks, particularly at those that are SIFIs. Approval of the candidate put forward by the bank is anything but assured. Candidates must undergo extensive pre-screening as well as pass an interview with the supervisor before the latter will approve the appointment. Candidates that do not pass muster must withdraw, either voluntarily or at the behest of the supervisor.[2]

Good governance

The next element in the sharper supervision program is to assure that the good people selected as directors and executives actually exercise good governance. In particular, supervisors are looking to assure themselves that the bank has a sound and sustainable business model, a robust risk appetite framework and a well-functioning, mutually rein-forcing "three lines" of defence system (line management, risk management/compliance and internal audit).

Reviewing business models

Assessing a bank's business model now figures prominently on the supervisory agenda.[3] Supervisors are in effect asking the bank the same type of questions that the bank itself would ask a corporate borrower that approaches it for a loan or for a guarantee. Does the bank have a strategy that could lead to success, and is the bank likely to be able to implement that strategy successfully, particularly in a stressed economic environment? As the bank's board and management de facto consider the answers to these questions to be yes, the supervisor's review of the bank's business model is in effect a "judgment on judgment."[4]

Controlling risk appetite

To judge whether or not the bank can implement a sound strategy successfully, the pro-active, forward-looking supervisor will review the bank's risk appetite framework (RAF) (see "Risk governance" in Chapter 2). In particular, the supervisor will want to assure itself that the bank has measures in place to keep its risk appetite within its risk capacity, even during stress.

In assessing how banks control risk appetite, supervisors will pay particular attention to how the bank cascades or allocates overall risk appetite for the group down to partic-ular lines of business and to particular legal vehicles. This will include a review of how the bank sets limits as well as how it monitors and enforces adherence to limits for credit and market risk. The supervisor will also assess how the bank controls operational and reputational risk. This "bottoms-up" view should be robust in its own right (especially for each of the group's principal legal vehicles) and consistent with the "tops-down" view set at group level for the institution as a whole.

To assure that banks base such measures on a sound foundation, supervisors are also insisting that banks improve the integrity and consistency of their data. In particular, supervisors of G-SIBs are demanding that banks make progress against the targets set by the Basel Committee for improved data management (see "Strengthening risk data" in Chapter 2), especially in connection with stress testing (see "Capital planning" later).

Establishing three lines of defence

Finally, the supervisor's review of governance will include a review of the bank's risk culture, in particular whether the bank in fact has three lines of defence (line management, risk management/compliance and internal audit) and whether each of these is doing what it should to limit and control risk.[5]

The litmus test for risk culture is line management. Does this in fact function as a first line of defence, or is line management focused solely on revenues and returns? This is the key question that supervisors are likely to put to banks. The supervisor will be looking for the bank to demonstrate that the front office "owns" the risk, that it views risk as the core of what a bank has to manage and that it actively strives to achieve the proper balance between return and risk.

The second line of defence is risk management and compliance. Here, supervisors are likely to ask:

- Is risk management setting and controlling limits in line with the bank's overall targets for risk and return so that the bank remains within its risk appetite and does not exhaust its risk capacity?

- Does risk management have a role to play in key decisions of business strategy, or do they just get involved after the fact?
- Can compliance assure that the bank is adhering to all the relevant rules and regulations in each of the jurisdictions in which the bank operates? If a breach does occur, is it promptly remedied and does the bank draw the appropriate lessons?
- Is compliance identifying issues which could become concerns in the future and taking steps to mitigate those risks?

The third line of defence is internal audit (IA). Here, supervisors are likely to ask:

- Is IA covering all the major risks the bank takes?
- Is IA testing the quality of the risk governance process and reporting findings to the board?
- Is IA discovering the right issues?
- Is management recommending the right remedies and implementing them promptly?

To test whether the three lines of defence are working as they should, supervisors are increasingly requiring that banks conduct "front-to-back" reviews of particular lines of business. Motivation for commissioning these reviews has been the series of losses arising in trading operations as well as the series of compliance breaches with respect to LIBOR, anti-money laundering, payment protection insurance and sales of mortgage securities. Such losses, settlements and fines have become so large that they represent a threat, not only to the bank's reputation, but to its ability to continue to meet capital requirements.

In addition, supervisors are stepping up cooperation with banks' external auditors, both to improve the quality of audits for banks generally as well as to engage in dialogue with the external auditor of individual banks on issues and concerns specific to that bank.[6] In some jurisdictions the external auditor has a duty to inform the supervisor of any emerging concerns that the auditor may have so that the supervisor may consider taking action promptly.[7]

Capital, liquidity and recovery planning

Assuring good governance is just the start of pro-active, forward-looking supervision. Increasingly, supervisors are acting to ensure that good governance generates good results. The principal means to this end are capital, liquidity and recovery planning so that the bank can survive even under extreme stress.

Capital planning

Supervisors use capital planning regimes to assure themselves that the bank will have enough capital, even under stress, to support its business activities, especially lending to small- to medium-sized enterprises (SMEs) and households.[8] To this end, the most active, forward-looking supervisors have undertaken a four-pronged program. This includes (i) accelerating adherence to the Basel minimums; (ii) setting individual capital guidance; (iii) initiating stress tests; and (iv) requiring supervisory approval to pay dividends or make cash distributions.

Accelerating adherence to Basel The 2010 agreement establishing Basel III envisioned a relatively long transition period to the new requirements. Full adherence to the new standards was not required until 2019. However, the market soon began to judge banks on the basis of the final, fully implemented rules. Supervisors soon followed suit, often using the stress test (see later) as a mechanism to accelerate adoption of the harder definition of capital and the higher minimum CET1 capital standards. In some cases, notably the United Kingdom, supervisors mandated early adherence to the leverage standard.

Setting individual capital guidance   In addition to accelerating the implementation of the tougher Basel III standards, some supervisors, again notably the United Kingdom, set individual capital guidance for each bank as well as an individual capital planning buffer.[9] This frequently results in add-ons to the minimum requirements to reflect risks that are not fully covered under Pillar I and/or to offset weaknesses in governance and/or data integrity.

Stress testing   Stress testing serves as a basis for capital planning. Supervisors set an economic stress scenario and examine how the bank would fare under such a scenario. In some cases (e.g., the United States) the supervisor itself conducts the test: it runs data on the banks' portfolios through models built by the supervisor. In others, the bank runs the test using its own models (but the supervisor's scenario).[10]

To assure that the stress test starts from a firm foundation, some jurisdictions (e.g., the Eurozone under the Single Supervision mechanism [SSM]) require that banks submit to an asset quality review prior to the stress test. This is to assure that banks are currently in good condition and to avoid the risk that "garbage in, garbage out" phenomenon will invalidate the results of the stress test.[11]

However, the key feature in each stress test is the target capital ratio – the ratio that banks have to meet under stress, if they are to pass the test. In general, supervisors have set the target ratio at a level considerably higher than the minimum called for under the Basel III transition arrangements. This has effectively accelerated the implementation of the final Basel III ratios.

For those banks that do not meet the target ratio, the supervisor will demand that the bank propose a series of management actions to correct the situation. These actions can include reduction in asset growth, the sale of or exit from certain lines of business, limits on cash bonuses or the issuance of new capital. The supervisor then reviews whether the proposed actions are likely to bring the bank's capital up to the "target stressed ratio" within the near future. If so, the supervisor approves the plan. If not, the supervisor sends the bank back to the drawing board and it may also consider initiating more formal intervention.

Supervisory approval of dividends and distributions. As a final stage in a stress test, supervisors examine whether the bank has an adequate capital planning buffer so that it is likely to be able to meet the target stressed ratio without adjustments to its business plan and without alterations to its plans to pay dividends and/or make distributions. Banks that have an adequate buffer receive a green light to pay dividends or make distributions in line with their plans. Banks that do not have an adequate buffer may not pay dividends or make distributions – a sanction that is proving to be a very effective supervisory tool to induce banks to mitigate risk.

Liquidity planning

As emphasised earlier, liquidity is the lifeblood of any bank, and liquidity planning is accordingly an important component of prudent management. Liquidity regulation aims to assure that banks limit their liquidity risk and that they maintain a buffer of liquid assets that they can draw upon to meet short-term outflows if inflows do not materialise as expected.

However, the supervisory focus extends beyond merely assuring that banks comply with liquidity regulation. The pro-active, forward-looking supervisor will also want to assure itself that the bank complies with the overall principles for sound liquidity management.[12] In particular, the supervisor will wish to assure itself that the bank has in place a robust contingency funding plan (CFP) that will allow the bank to raise funds even under conditions where one or more markets are closed entirely or closed to the bank in question. The collateral budget outlined earlier (see "Measuring liquidity risks" in Chapter 2) should be an important input into the CFP, for it will provide a basis for determining the amount of unencumbered assets that the bank might have available to sell or pledge to lenders.[13]

Of particular interest to supervisors and central banks is the degree to which the bank's CFP involves tapping central bank facilities. Those CFPs that envisage early and/or extensive reliance on central bank facilities are likely to be judged less satisfactory than those that rely primarily on private sources of funding. For CFPs that do involve recourse to central bank facilities, supervisors and central banks will want to assure that such recourse does not involve emergency liquidity assistance but is restricted to normal facilities such as discount window lending. Supervisors and/or central banks may also wish the bank whose CFP relies on recourse to such facilities to pre-position eligible collateral with the central bank and/or make arrangements with the central bank so that the central bank could rapidly take a charge over the bank's assets.[14]

Recovery planning

Recovery planning pulls together capital and liquidity planning. It outlines the measures the bank could take to recover from extreme stress. This enables the supervisor to assess the bank's resiliency. The emphasis in a recovery plan is on developing a number of options that the bank could implement relatively rapidly, each of which would be large enough to "move the needle" and lead to a significant improvement in the bank's capital and/or liquidity ratio.[15]

Triggering the recovery plan in a timely manner is a key to its successful implementation. Many options, such as the sale of a business or the raising of new capital, take time to execute. Although advance planning (e.g., having draft documentation or shelf registration for capital issuance in place) can reduce these time frames, a certain minimum will be required for successful execution at a "normal" price. The closer the bank comes to the point of non-viability, the more likely it is that it will be forced to conduct what amounts to a fire sale – a process that is unlikely to result in the bank's recovery. Consequently, the supervisor will want to assure that the bank has timely information about its actual and prospective condition, that the bank takes a realistic view of its condition and that it has a bias towards taking corrective action promptly rather than remaining in denial and/or hoping that improvements in economic conditions will restore the bank to health.

Supervisory intervention

The reports and plans that banks submit to the supervisor are the raw material of supervision. They enable the supervisor to monitor the bank's condition. But supervision is more than monitoring – to be effective, the supervisor must intervene where it judges that the bank is taking undue risk and/or veering toward failure.[16]

To do so, the forward-looking, pro-active supervisor will classify banks according to their distance from failure. As the distance to resolution shortens, the supervisor will step up the intensity of supervision, particularly at systemically important institutions. To deepen its understanding of specific risk issues, the supervisor may commission skilled-person reviews. As banks come closer to the danger zone, the supervisor may mandate that the bank take corrective action, including without limitation restricting certain activities, reducing certain risks and/or lowering leverage. The supervisor will also require the bank to refresh and prepare to trigger its recovery plan as well as take steps to prepare the bank for resolution, if necessary.

Classifying banks

The first step towards pro-active supervision is to classify banks according to their distance from the point of non-viability or the point at which the bank would fail to meet threshold conditions. This will depend on general economic conditions as well as on a number of bank-specific factors, including the bank's risk capacity and its risk appetite, as well as how resilient the bank might be, if it invoked its recovery plan (see Figure 3.1). The closer the bank is to the point of non-viability, the more intensive and intrusive the supervisor will be. Indeed, that is the whole point of supervision – to induce or force the bank to take steps that will push it out of the danger zone.

Ideally, the supervisor can induce the bank to take the steps that the supervisor deems necessary. After all, the board and management of the bank should also be keen to avert failure. And, in most cases the supervisor's suggestions are the same type of recommendations (e.g., "raise new capital") that the bank itself would make to a corporate borrower who was in danger of breaching its loan covenants. However, the supervisor can also be quite persuasive because it also has a big stick. Should the bank refuse to take the remediation measures that the supervisor considers necessary, the supervisor can effectively use a variety of intervention tools to force the bank to do so.

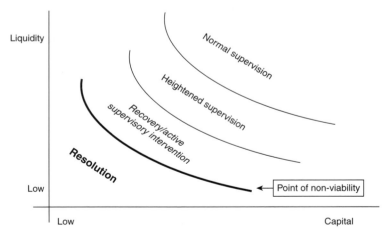

Figure 3.1   Distance to resolution drives supervisory classification

Skilled-person reviews

The first of these tools is a skilled-person review. This can shed light on a particular risk issue, either across firms or at a particular firm. In such a review the supervisor mandates that the bank hire a skilled person at the bank's expense to take a "deep dive" into a particular issue. The supervisor sets the agenda for the review, and the skilled-person reports the results to the supervisor. The review should identify any shortcomings and develop a corrective action program for the bank to implement. Upon confirmation of the skilled-person's report by the supervisor, the bank obligates itself to implement the corrective action program within a certain time frame.

Risk mitigation program

If the supervisor's concerns relate to the bank's overall risk, it can formally mandate that the bank agree to an overall risk mitigation program. This commits the bank to certain actions, such as the placing limits on certain activities or lines of business, reducing risk exposures and/or raising capital ratios within a tight time frame, and subjects it to more frequent reporting and monitoring. Under a risk mitigation program the supervisor may also require the bank to refresh and prepare to trigger its recovery plan as well as take steps to facilitate resolution. Should the bank not comply, it would become subject to more severe sanctions, including the possibility that the supervisor would force the bank to replace members of management and/or the board of directors.

Placing the bank into resolution

Should the bank, despite the efforts of its management and the supervisor, reach the point of non-viability, the supervisor must be prepared to "pull the trigger" and put the bank into resolution. That requires that the supervisor have a viable resolution plan, one that will avoid costs to the taxpayer and limit any adverse impact on financial markets or the economy as a whole (see Chapter 4).

If the supervisor has such a resolution plan, the bank must reckon that the supervisor would actually use it, rather than exercise forbearance, should the bank reach the point of non-viability. This should make the bank's management and board more receptive to the supervisor's recommendations in the heightened supervision or recovery phases as to how the bank might rectify its condition.

In sum, micro-prudential supervision seeks to assure that a bank will remain in good condition, that it will in fact observe the covenants imposed by regulation and that it will put into resolution in a timely fashion any bank that reaches the point of non-viability.

Macro-prudential supervision

However, micro-prudential supervision can only go so far in preventing crises. Indeed in looking back at the crisis, many observers concluded that policymakers had focused prior to the crisis too narrowly on their own specific mandate: central banks on controlling inflation, bank supervisors on whether or not banks were observing the rules, securities regulators on disclosure and market conduct and so on. No authority considered itself responsible for looking at the picture as a whole. Consequently no one did, and no one felt it was their job to put a stop to the excesses that were developing in the market. This contributed to the crisis.

To assure that someone would in fact look at the picture as a whole, identify risks to the financial system and the economy at large, and take measures to mitigate these risks, policymakers embraced the concept of macro-prudential supervision and set up bodies to exercise this responsibility. These bodies in turn have initiated a broad agenda that includes consideration of measures to (i) reduce or even reverse pro-cyclicality in regulation; (ii) control shadow banking; (iii) assure that financial market infrastructures remain robust; (iv) assure that all systemically important firms are subject to prudential regulation; and (v) make systemically important firms, especially banks, resolvable.

The architecture of macro-prudential supervision

At the top of the macro-prudential policy apparatus sits the Financial Stability Board (FSB), a committee consisting of representatives from finance ministries, central banks and supervisory authorities from the world's principal economies. In 2008 the heads of state of the G-20 charged the FSB with the responsibility to oversee the global financial system as well as orchestrate, together with industry-specific standard-setters such as the Basel Committee for Banking Supervision, the reform of regulation and supervision, especially for G-SIFIs.[17] Thanks in no small measure to this G-20 mandate and to the continuing support from finance ministers and heads of state, the FSB has been extremely effective, as evidenced in its periodic reports to the G-20, in creating and implementing an ambitious reform agenda.[18]

Individual countries, as well as the EU, have also established bodies similar to the FSB to exercise macro-prudential supervision. In the United States, the Secretary of the Treasury chairs the Financial Stability Oversight Council (FSOC), a body that brings together the various federal agencies charged with supervision of financial institutions and financial markets, including the Federal Reserve (in its capacity as central bank as well as supervisor), the FDIC, the Securities Exchange Commission (SEC) and the Commodities Futures Trading Commission (CFTC).[19] The EU has established the European Systemic Risk Board (ESRB).[20] The President of the European Central Bank chairs the ESRB. Its members are the heads of the national central banks in the 28 Member States in the EU, together with the heads of the national authorities for supervision. The United Kingdom

Safe to Fail

has established the Financial Policy Committee (FPC) in parallel to the Monetary Policy Committee (MPC). The Governor of the Bank of England chairs the FPC, and each of the Bank's Deputy Governors is a member as is the head of the Financial Conduct Authority. Like the MPC, the FPC also contains outside members, and like the MPC the FPC has real power to set policy. If the FPC makes a recommendation to the PRA, the PRA must either comply or explain.[21]

Reducing or reversing pro-cyclicality in regulation

Banking is inherently a pro-cyclical business. As the economy expands and contracts, so does credit. The rationale for macro-prudential supervision of credit rests on the premise that credit does not merely reflect the economic cycle; it amplifies or even causes the economic cycle. Overextension of credit during the upswing is said to lead to overheating of the economy, whilst contraction of credit during the downturn to delay or even derail the recovery.[22]

Consequently macro-prudential supervision attempts to taper credit expansion during the boom and to stimulate credit extension at the trough of the cycle, principally by adjusting banks' capital. During the upswing of the business cycle, if the macro-prudential supervisor comes to the conclusion that "excessive" credit growth poses a threat to economic and/or financial stability it can instruct the bank supervisor to impose a counter-cyclical capital buffer of up to 2.5 per cent of risk-weighted assets on top of the capital conservation buffer. The rationale is that this will make lending more "expensive" and cause the lender to contract credit or at least moderate its rate of expansion. Ideally, this moderation of the rate of credit expansion would enable the economy to delay or even avoid entirely the turning point from upswing to downswing.[23]

If the problem in the upswing is too easy credit (and therefore overextension of credit), the problem in the downswing is too little credit. If banks are overly restrictive, worthwhile projects may not get financed and economic activity may stall, particularly if banks are the predominant source of credit in the economy and borrowers lack access to capital markets. Here, the diagnosis is that banks lack the inclination to lend because they lack the capacity to lend. At the trough of the cycle, banks are short on capital and reluctant to raise new equity, especially if the bank is concerned that the due diligence required as part of the equity issuance process might reveal that assets were overvalued and additional write-downs or provisions required.

At very low levels of equity, such reluctance is entirely rational – the economic benefit of issuing new equity goes predominantly to the bank's creditors, a phenomenon known in corporate finance as "debt overhang."[24] In such a situation, each bank will, whilst waiting for the recovery, refrain from issuing new equity and may refrain from making new loans to creditworthy borrowers. It will also seek to refrain from taking write-offs. Vis-à-vis borrowers in arrears, a bank with its own "debt overhang" is likely to implement a policy of forbearance toward borrowers in arrears. Also known as "extend and pretend," this policy in effect represents a triumph of hope (namely that a possible economic recovery will restore the creditworthiness of the borrower) over experience (namely that borrowers in arrears are very likely to stay that way, even if the economy does recover).

The "macro-prudential" solution is to impose "transparency" on the banks. Rather than exercise forbearance, the supervisor actually bears down on the banks. To this end the macro-prudential supervisor may instruct the micro-prudential supervisor to do what the micro-prudential supervisor should in any event be periodically doing, namely, conducting a balance sheet assessment (BSA) or asset quality review (AQR) of the banks under its supervision, coupled perhaps with a stress test. In substance, such a BSA/AQR is a very comprehensive version of the due diligence exercise that the bank would have to undergo before it could raise new equity. If this review estimates that the bank has a short-fall of capital against the target level it would need to survive under stress, the supervisor will instruct the bank in question to file and execute a plan to bring its capital up to the target level and to do this without cutting back on lending, at least to creditworthy domestic borrowers. Provided the banks can actually raise the required capital in a timely fashion, such macro/micro-prudential measures will assure that the banks at least have the capacity to lend.[25]

However, the jury is still out on whether these macro-prudential measures will actually help tame the economic cycle. Although the prescription has been quite definite, the diagnosis may be faulty. Accordingly, the prescription need not cure the problem. Indeed, it may aggravate the problem (see Appendix: Does Credit Create the Cycle?).

Control shadow banking

Authorities have also moved to control so-called shadow banking.[26] This involves placing restrictions on banks' ability to conduct banking in the shadows as well as on the ability of non-bank financial institutions to act as if they were banks. In addition, the authorities are developing rules to control the use of collateral, as this is by and large essential to the funding and business models that shadow banking employs.

Eliminating banking in the shadows

Stricter rules regarding consolidation of off-balance sheet vehicles and tougher limits on large exposures practically eliminate the ability of banks to operate in the shadows via conduits and structured investment vehicles. Prior to the crisis many banks had created such vehicles as part of what might be called an "acquire to arbitrage" strategy.[27] Although the sponsoring bank provided management and a liquidity back-stop to such vehicles, under technical accounting stand-ards (particularly US GAAP) the sponsoring bank did not have to include the assets and liabilities of such vehicles into the bank's consolidated accounts. As a result, such vehicles were not subject to capital requirements. The new rules force such consolidation at least for the purposes of calculating capital requirements.

Controlling shadow banking: the case of money market mutual funds

Money market mutual funds (MMMFs) with a fixed net asset value (NAV) are very significant participants in the money market and provide large amounts of short-term funding to financial institutions and other firms. MMMFs pose a systemic risk, because they are – as far as the investors in the funds are concerned – economically equivalent to banks.

Like banks MMMFs are exposed to the risk that investors will run on the fund. Technically, the funds issue shares (equity) to investors, and investors are exposed to the risk that the shares in the fund will decline in value. However, fund sponsors generally market the shares as equivalent to deposits. The shares have a constant NAV (usually $1 or €1) and fund sponsors generally advertise that the shares are redeemable upon demand at the fixed NAV. In other words, the fund shares are equivalent to a demand deposit with a variable interest rate.

In theory, the diversification of the fund's assets as well as the limitation on the riskiness and maturity of the fund's investments should combine to assure that the fund will not "break the buck" – that the fund can maintain its fixed NAV. In fact, however, there is a risk that the MMMF will have to do so. If it becomes known or perceived that the MMMF will have to break the buck, investors have every incentive to redeem their shares as quickly as possible in full at the fixed NAV. If such a run does develop, this increases the probability that the MMMF will in fact break the buck. And, if once one MMMF does, this raises the probability that there will be a run on all MMMFs with fixed NAVs. As such a general run could destabilise financial markets, central banks might feel compelled to provide support to MMMFs (as the US Federal Reserve did in 2008 in the wake of the Lehmans failure, when the Prime Reserve Fund "broke the buck"). If investors in MMMFs began to take such intervention for granted, this would create a situation akin to "too big to fail" for G-SIBs. That would compound the systemic risk posed by MMMFs with fixed NAVs.

To nip this possibility in the bud, authorities in the United States and EU are considering (in line with FSB recommendations) requiring MMMFs with fixed NAVs to switch to a variable NAV or to impose combination of a NAV buffer (prudent valuation adjustment) and "minimum balance at risk" requirement.[28] Either of these proposals would end the systemic risk posed by MMMFs – but would also radically change the MMMF business model. Accordingly, there has been considerable resistance to the proposed changes, and neither the United States nor the EU has as yet issued a final rule in this area.

Controlling the repo market

Collateral is the lifeblood of shadow banks, such as hedge funds, as well as non-bank financial institutions such as broker-dealers. They predominantly finance themselves through secured borrowing. The investments that such firms make serve as the collateral for the loans that they receive from banks and other lenders.

Much of this borrowing takes the form of repurchase agreements (repos) in which the "borrower" sells securities to the "lender" with a commitment from the borrower to repurchase the securities from the lender at a fixed price upon the maturity of the repo agreement. This fixed repurchase price exceeds the initial price at which the lender bought the securities from the borrower – the difference is effectively the interest on the loan. Should the borrower not buy the securities back at the agreed time at the agreed price, the lender has the right to sell the securities received from the borrower and use the proceeds to satisfy the obligation of the borrower. If the proceeds exceed the debt, the lender returns the excess to the borrower. If the proceeds are insufficient to retire the debt, the lender has an unsecured claim on the borrower for the difference. To assure that the sale of the securities will generate enough proceeds to satisfy the debt, the lender usually limits the advance rate on the securities bought from the borrower. In other words, the lender imposes a "haircut" on the market value of the securities bought from the borrower.

But the repo market has three weak spots, and regulators have proposed remedies to correct each of them. [29] First, haircuts could prove insufficient, so that the lender would be unsecured, rather than secured for some portion of its exposure to the borrower, if the borrower failed to repurchase the securities as scheduled. The FSB has therefore proposed that lenders be required to impose minimum haircuts on securities taken as collateral. This protects lenders and lessens the potential for sudden increases in collateral demands from lenders as market conditions and/or the borrower's creditworthiness deteriorate.

A second weak spot stems from re-hypothecation, or the multiple use of the same collateral in what amounts to a financing chain.[30] This poses significant issues, particularly where the original borrower has used client assets as the basis for borrowing to finance its own position (see Box 3.1). Accordingly the FSB has recommended that limits be placed of such activity and that clients be kept more fully informed as to the risks they incur, when they permit re-hypothecation of their assets.

Box 3.1   How re-hypothecation works

This risk arises if a client (C) grants the bank (B) at which it holds its securities account the right to re-use or re-hypothecate the securities that the client C had pledged to the bank as collateral in connection with a margin loan that C had received from B. If B then uses the collateral received from C to obtain financing from Lender L, client C will be at risk if bank B defaults on its loan from Lender L.

A concrete example illustrates why this is the case. Bank B sells the securities received from Client C to Lender L under a repurchase agreement. If Bank B cannot repurchase the securities from Lender L at the agreed price at the agreed time, Lender L will liquidate the securities received from Bank B. This extinguishes Lender L's claim on Bank B, but it means that Bank B no longer has Client C's securities to return to Client C. Client C has an unsecured claim on Bank B. This will be reduced via offset by any loan that Client C may have had from Bank B, but Client C will at a minimum be exposed to Bank B for the amount of any haircut (excess of value of securities over amount of the loan) that Bank B had imposed.

These risks magnify as the collateral chain lengthens. There is no inherent reason why the chain should stop at the second link. Lender L can use the original borrower's securities as collateral to borrow from Lender M. Lender M can in turn use these same securities to borrow from Lender N and so on. A default at any point along the chain will have knock-on effects throughout the chain.

The third weak spot in the repo market is the "market" itself, especially in the United States.[31] There the market is largely conducted on a so-called tri-party basis. At the hub of the system are two banks that bring together lenders and borrowers. The authorities and market participants have identified and are working to mitigate three sources of systemic risk: (i) an over-reliance on intraday credit,[32] (ii) poor risk management practices at both lenders and borrowers,[33] and (iii) fire sales of assets.[34]

Assure financial market infrastructures are robust

At the very core of the financial system stand a series of financial market infrastructures (FMIs): payment systems, securities settlements systems and central counterparties. Collectively, these FMIs constitute the "plumbing" of the financial system, and financial stability depends critically on this plumbing working well at all times (see Chapter 1).

Indeed, FMIs are "single points of failure" in the financial system. They are inherently systemic and the largest are certainly important – a fact that systemic risk boards have started to confirm via formal designation of FMIs as SIFIs.[35] Should an FMI fail, each of its participants could be adversely affected. Participants would not only be unable to use the FMI to process payments, settle securities trades or conduct derivative transactions, but one or more of the FMI's participants could also suffer losses to capital and/or drains on liquidity that could in turn threaten the participant's own survival.

For this reason FMIs need to be robust. According to the Committee on Payment and Securities Settlement Systems (CPSS) and the International Organisation of Securities Commissions (IOSCO), "robust" means the ability to survive the simultaneous failure of two or more of their largest participants.[36] To demonstrate that they can in fact do so, FMIs will be required to submit recovery plans to their supervisors for review and authorities should develop plans on how they might resolve an FMI, if the FMI's recovery plan fails to restore it to health.[37]

Assure all systemically important firms are subject to prudential regulation

Banks are not the only SIFIs. Non-bank financial institutions can also be systemically important. If so, they should, according to the G-20 be subject to prudential regulation and required to develop recovery and resolution plans so that their failure would not significantly disrupt financial markets or the economy at large and would not lead to the provision of taxpayer support.[38]

This is already under way for FMIs (see "Assure financial market infrastructures are robust" earlier). The question is whether certain other non-bank financial institutions – insurance companies, non-bank financial companies, asset managers – could also be designated as systemic and therefore subject to more intensive supervision and as well as to a requirement that they maintain higher loss-absorbing capacity.

In concept, the answer is yes. If an institution is systemically important, it should be subject to prudential supervision. In practice, the FSB has designated nine insurance companies as globally systemically important and will reach a determination with respect to reinsurance companies in 2014.[39] However, neither non-bank finance companies nor asset managers have as yet been designated as systemic, even in the United States, where such institutions play a significant role in the financial system.[40] Nor have the government sponsored enterprises, such as Fannie Mae and Freddie Mac, despite their undoubted systemic importance and significant contribution to causing the financial crisis.[41]

Make systemically important firms, especially banks, resolvable

The final item in the systemic risk board's agenda is to end too big to fail – to make systemically important financial institutions resolvable (see Chapter 4). This has far-reaching implications for firms, for finance and for the economy at large (see Chapter 5).

Conduct regulation and supervision

In addition to assuring that banks remain in good condition, regulation and supervision should assure that banks maintain good conduct in their dealings with both individuals and institutions.

Banks have not. Their failing to do so has compromised the reputation of individual firms and the industry as a whole; prompted payments (fines, settlements and restitution to customers) large enough to threaten firms' ability to rebuild capital; and, in some cases, exposed firms to criminal sanctions. In response, policymakers have intensified enforcement of existing regulations, tightened the rules and augmented supervision.

Wholesale markets

This response covers both wholesale and retail markets. In wholesale markets, regulators have focused on assuring the integrity of financial markets, both through enforcement actions and revision of regulation. Four areas are the centre of official attention: (i) the manipulation of benchmarks, (ii) sales of mortgage-backed securities, (iii) insider trading and (iv) anti-money laundering. Together, failings in these areas constitute a damning indictment of culture at major banks. They also amply demonstrate the need for remediation and reform.

Manipulation of benchmarks

Financial markets rely heavily on benchmarks to set a reference price for various contracts and markets. To set these benchmarks, the compiler receives submissions of rates or prices from market participants, inputs the data into the formula for the benchmark and publishes the result. This procedure can be contaminated, if market participants collude with one another and/or the submissions are based on indicative rates rather than actual transactions.

That is what happened in the case of LIBOR. Traders at a number of major banks colluded in their submission of rates to the benchmark compiler, the British Banking Association.[42] Fines to date in connection with LIBOR exceed \$5 billion. Further fines are likely, as are settlements or penalties in connection with civil lawsuits filed by investors and counterparties in the United States and a number of other jurisdictions.

In addition to continuing enforcement actions in connection with past LIBOR violations, the authorities have initiated similar investigations with respect to alleged fixing of other benchmarks, such as foreign exchange. Finally, authorities have moved to reform LIBOR[43] in particular and to set principles for benchmarks in general. These focus on improving the methodology used to create benchmarks and strengthening the governance used in administering the benchmark process.[44]

Sales of mortgage-backed securities

When underwriting and distributing securities to investors, banks and the issuer must attest that the prospectus is accurate. If this proves not to be the case, the underwriter and/or the issuer may be subject to fines as well as liable for damages under civil lawsuits.

That is essentially what happened with respect to the sales of mortgage-backed securities (MBS) in the United States. Prospectuses contained the statement that banks originating the mortgages underlying the MBS had conformed to certain underwriting principles such as assuring that the loan-to-value and/or loan-to-income ratio did not exceed a certain level. However, this was not always the case, especially where the originating bank had relied upon mortgage brokers to conduct appraisals and/or check documentation of the borrower's income. The MBS therefore contained significantly more substandard loans with a default and recovery experience that was far worse than had been expected (and indicated in the prospectus). As this became apparent, the price of MBS fell, resulting in losses to guarantors and investors, who in turn sought to recoup some portion of their loss by suing the banks that had originated the underlying mortgages and/or underwritten the MBS. To date, banks have incurred over $100 billion in costs (fines, legal fees and customer restitution) in settlement of these lawsuits.[45]

In addition to continuing enforcement action against various banks, the authorities have instituted a number of reforms to prevent such abuses from recurring.[46] First, banking regulators have instituted a retention requirement in connection with asset-backed securities in general. Banks originating or underwriting such securities must retain a portion of the security or the underlying mortgages in their own portfolio. This is intended to align their interests with those of investors and to induce the underwriting banks to exercise control over each stage of the origination process, including steps that may be undertaken by third parties such as mortgage brokers. In addition, capital requirements relating to securitisation have been revised to remove artificial inducements to securitise loans and assure that investments in securitisations receive an adequate risk weighting (see "Increasing capital requirements" Chapter 2).

Reform of credit rating agencies

Second, the authorities have reformed regulation of the rating agencies. Prior to the crisis the rating agencies granted what amounted to a seal of approval to securitisation issues, particularly the senior tranches, which frequently received the highest (AAA) ratings – ratings that conferred a lower risk weight on the security for the purposes of bank capital regulation. Initially, the rating agencies had run a check on some of the key statements in the prospectus (such as the LTV and LTI ratios mentioned earlier) by examining a sample of the files for the loans underlying the MBS. However, as time progressed, rating agencies sampled fewer and fewer loans and the check became less effective.[47]

In response, authorities have taken steps to reduce the reliance that regulation places on ratings and to subject rating agencies themselves to regulation and supervision.[48] The United States and the EU have already taken concrete steps toward eliminating the mechanistic reliance of ratings in capital regulation – the intent is to force banks, if they are to use models, to make and document their own judgements on risk and to resort to a supervisor-determined standardised approach, if they are not. With respect to the rating agencies themselves, they must henceforth be more transparent about their processes and methodology as well as take steps to manage better the conflicts of interest to which they may be exposed. As a result, rating agencies may need to re-examine the issuer-pays business model that they currently use.

Insider trading

A prohibition on insider trading is central to the integrity and fairness of financial markets. Persons with access to price-sensitive, non-public information should not trade on that information. Nor should they disclose such information to others (unless they are authorised to do so and the recipient is bound by the duty of confidentiality). Disclosure of such information should come from the company at the appropriate time and be disseminated to all investors simultaneously.

This has not always been the case. In particular, a number of high-profile hedge-fund investors have engaged in insider trading.[49] For the individuals concerned, it means sizeable fines and/or penalties and, in some cases, a period in jail. For the firms at which they worked, the loss of reputation may be more damaging than the monetary loss associated with the penalties imposed. In the case of hedge funds this loss of reputation may extend more broadly from firms convicted of insider trading to hedge-fund managers as a whole. After all, if most if not all of a convicted fund's excess return ("alpha") is due to trading on insider information, the suspicion may arise that insider trading is also the source of excess returns at other funds with outsize performance.

Anti-money laundering

Denying terrorists and criminals, such as drug dealers, access to the banking system is considered essential to the preservation of national and international security. Accordingly jurisdictions have introduced – in line with recommendations from the Financial Action Task Force (FATF) – regulations requiring banks to "know your customer" (KYC), to block payments to/from organisations or individuals suspected of terrorist activity and to report to the authorities suspicious transactions.[50]

In many cases, banks have not met their obligations. They have failed to implement KYC policies, failed to adhere to sanctions and/or failed to report suspicious transactions. This has resulted in fines for the banks concerned and a requirement that banks complete remediation programs. Some banks are under so-called deferred prosecution agreements: failure to remediate the issue could lead to the authorities subjecting the bank to criminal indictment. That in turn could adversely affect the ability of the bank to transact with customers, attract funding or retain its banking license.

In addition to pursuing enforcement actions and investigations, regulators have tightened the rules. In particular, "know your customer" (KYC) has been extended to "know your customer's customer" (KYCC). Correspondent banks are no longer able to place complete reliance on the AML and KYC procedures of the bank where the originator or ultimate recipient of a cross-border payment may have his account. Before executing a payment request, the correspondent bank must undertake its own review of the procedures of the originating or recipient bank and seek to identify suspicious transactions. This significantly raises the cost of executing cross-border payments, so that a number of banks active in international payments have decided to pare back their transfers to or from particular banks or even entire countries.

Retail markets and consumer protection

Consumer protection also figures prominently on the reform agenda.[51] The focus is on assuring that consumers get adequate and accurate information on which to base their decisions, that financial institutions treat customers fairly and that they respond promptly to complaints and offer consumers appropriate redress.

The implementation of this agenda is occurring predominantly at national level. The United States and the United Kingdom are perhaps furthest advanced. The United States has set up the Consumer Financial Protection Bureau to provide more vigorous enforcement of the extensive consumer protection laws and regulations that exist in the United States.[52] In the United Kingdom the Financial Conduct Authority has the mandate to provide appropriate protection to consumers and to assure that competition acts in the interest of consumers.[53]

The intent is to assure that retail customers get a fair deal and, ideally, a good outcome. In numerous cases in the past, consumers have gotten neither. For example, in the United

Kingdom, banks have mis-sold pensions, payment protection insurance and investment products, such as split capital investment trusts. This has resulted in billions of pounds in fines and restitution to customers – amounts sufficiently large to compromise banks' capital plans.

More importantly, such conduct violations have – together with the offenses banks have committed in the wholesale market – undermined banks' reputation and diminished the trust that people have in their own bank and in the banking system at large. Moreover, banks' reputation has not necessarily touched bottom. Further evidence of banks' bad behaviour is likely to emerge as enforcement proceedings continue with respect to various "legacy" cases. Banks will be hard put to demonstrate that they have the correct culture in place, for bad habits are hard to break.

This loss of reputation has significant implications for banks' future. People and policymakers alike abhor the idea that taxpayer funds should be used to support the very banks that rig markets and abuse clients. That has to stop. Banks need to "clean up their act," and banks need to become resolvable (see Chapter 4). Otherwise, they are likely to be broken up (see Conclusion).

Summary

In sum, reform of supervision reinforces the reform of regulation. The contribution of supervision is twofold: it not only monitors the adherence of banks to regulatory requirements, it also takes a critical, forward look on banks' ability to remain in good condition, at the level both of the individual bank and the system as a whole. And if that forward look reveals risks to the viability of either the individual bank or the system as a whole, the supervisor should intervene to mitigate the risk. This will push the individual bank away from the point of non-viability, make it less likely to fail and contribute to financial stability.

Appendix: Does credit create the cycle?

Like all markets, the credit market reflects the interaction between supply and demand. But credit is an input to practically all other markets, so distortions in the credit market can have knock-on effects on the economy at large. If credit is priced too cheaply or granted on too generous terms, institutions and individuals will increase borrowing for investment and/or consumption. This in turn boosts spending and could lead to the economy "overheating." Conversely, if credit is priced too dearly, granted on too restrictive terms or rationed, institutions and individuals may not be able to finance planned investment and/or consumption. As a result, spending will decline and economic growth may sputter to a halt or even go into reverse – a phenomenon known as the debt-deflation cycle. Preventing the economy from veering off into either of these two extremes is one of the primary objectives of macroprudential supervision, and the rationale for the counter-cyclical bank capital measures described in the text.

But the premises for such policy are (i) a clear understanding and acceptance of what constitutes "normal" credit conditions, and (ii) a dominant role for banks in the provision of credit. Neither appears to be the case, and this creates the risk that counter-cyclical policies may over time simply become counter-bank policies.

From the vantage point of a prudently managed bank, the price at which the bank should be willing to extend credit should depend on the risk of the loan and be reflected in a spread over the risk-free rate for terms of equivalent maturity. The risk of the loan depends on the probability of default (PD) and loss given default (LGD). But both PD and LGD depend on expectations, first about the income that the borrower might have available to service its debt, and second about the value that the lender might realise if it had to sell the collateral that the borrower had pledged as security for the loan.

Such expectations on PD and LGD depend on how lenders estimate the economy will develop. This is generally an extrapolation of current trends, or possibly based on official forecasts, such as those from the central bank. Such methods are unlikely to identify turning points, particularly from upswing to downswing. [54]

As economic conditions improve, so generally do lenders' expectations of borrowers' future earnings as well as lenders' expectations of the recoveries that they might realise if the borrower were to default. Lenders may also take a view that borrowers' earnings are likely to remain more stable. Indeed, such expectations on the part of lenders are perfectly consistent with the base-line economic forecast that central banks and finance ministries are prone to give as a recovery takes hold. The improved income prospects of borrowers make borrowers more creditworthy, and this allows borrowers either to borrow the same amount on better terms or a larger amount on the same terms. What has changed is the condition of the borrower, not necessarily the credit standards of the bank. The result is an increase in the volume of credit and possibly an increase in the volume of credit relative to GDP, corporate earnings and/or household income.

Similarly, in the downswing, as economic conditions deteriorate, so generally do lenders' expectations of borrowers' future earnings as well as lenders' expectations of the recoveries that they might realise if the borrower were to default. Correspondingly, borrowers will have to pay higher rates to obtain the same amount of credit, or borrowers will have to reduce their outstanding debt to keep the same terms. The bank's credit standards have not changed. Nor has its propensity to lend. Its view of the client's condition has, based on the deterioration in the economic environment.

Expectations about the economy also drive the demand for credit. Firms invest in inventory, plant and equipment if they expect their revenues to grow, and that depends on how the economy develops. In a recession, or in uncertain environment with weak growth prospects, firms that are still earning good money are reluctant to invest. They tend to hoard cash or even repay debt, so that they can survive what might be hard times ahead. Firms that are already losing money are by definition reducing their equity and becoming less creditworthy. As their PDs rise, banks should – if they are to remain prudent – increase spreads, tighten terms and/or reduce the volume of credit to such firms.

Hence, the volume of credit will accelerate in the upswing and decelerate in the downswing of the business cycle, even though lenders' credit standards remain unchanged. What changes is (i) lenders' expectation of borrowers' capacity to repay, either from earnings or asset values; and (ii) borrower's demand for credit.

Credit therefore largely reflects the economic cycle. It does not necessarily cause or aggravate the economic cycle. To expect banks to counteract this normal process implicitly demands banks have an extraordinary level of clairvoyance about when the economy might reach a turning point, so that the bank would curtail credit as a boom progressed and extend credit in the downturn in anticipation of the recovery to come.

Macro-prudential supervision promises to give banks that clairvoyance, at least during the upswing of the cycle, by initiating a counter-cyclical buffer. But if this buffer applies only to banks, credit will not necessarily be curtailed. Borrowers can and very likely will access other sources of credit, such as securities markets. The growth in total credit need not diminish, even if the growth in bank credit does. For macro-prudential supervision to succeed in controlling total credit, the counter-cyclical measures would have to be aimed at borrowers, not banks.

4

Safe to Fail

Reforming resolution constitutes the second, and arguably more important, pillar of the reform program initiated by the G-20 in response to the crisis. This aims to make banks resolvable, so that the failure of a bank need not disrupt financial markets or the economy at large and so that investors, not taxpayers, bear the cost of bank failures. In other words, reform aims to make banks "safe to fail."

Authorities and banks have made considerable progress towards this goal. There is agreement on objectives and on the key attributes that resolution regimes should have, and key jurisdictions are putting such regimes in place. These contain an overall framework for resolution, and work is proceeding on filling in the details and on eliminating the remaining obstacles to resolution. This promises to make banks – including the G-SIBs at the heart of the global financial system – resolvable.

When is a bank resolvable?

Resolution reform aims

> to make feasible the resolution of financial institutions without severe systemic disruption and without exposing taxpayers to loss, while protecting vital economic functions through mechanisms which make it possible for shareholders and unsecured and uninsured creditors to absorb losses in a manner that respects the hierarchy of claims in liquidation.[1]

An institution is therefore resolvable if three conditions are met:

1. The institution can be readily recapitalised without recourse to taxpayer money.
2. The institution in resolution can continue to conduct normal[2] transactions with customers, ideally from the opening of business on the business day following the initiation of the resolution.
3. The resolution process itself does not significantly disrupt financial markets or the economy at large.

The resolution timeline

Resolution is akin to running a trauma centre at a hospital. In the background the institutional framework provides facilities and staffing, governs admission policy and sets overall policies and procedures. For each individual case the focus is first on stabilising the patient, and then, if that is successful, on rehabilitating the patient.

Bank resolution should follow a similar pattern. The resolution regime sets the framework. Actual resolution of a specific institution falls into three phases: pulling the trigger, stabilising the institution and restructuring the institution (see Figure 4.1). In effect, resolution for a G-SIB is a process whereby the authorities can put an institution that has fallen into a state of paralysis at the close of business on a Friday night (i) back on its feet by the opening of business on Monday so that it can conduct normal business operations; and (ii) back to full health some months later.

The resolution regime: the role of the resolution authority

To have the power to effect this transformation, the authorities require an appropriate resolution regime.[3] Such a regime

Safe to Fail

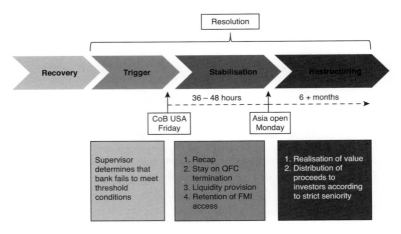

Figure 4.1   Resolution: tight time frames dictate advance planning

establishes the legal basis in which resolution takes place. The FSB has established the key attributes that such a regime should have, and the G-20 countries are making progress towards implementation (see Table 4.1), particularly in jurisdictions in which G-SIBs have their headquarters. However, significant gaps remain, especially with respect to the provision of liquidity to the bank-in-resolution and with respect to cross-border cooperation.

The United States, Switzerland and Japan already have legislation in place that meet practically all of the FSB standards, and the EU has in 2014 enacted the Banking Recovery and Resolution Directive (BRRD), which will apply across all 28 Member States, as well as putting the finishing touches to banking union for the Eurozone. The BRRD will establish a statutory bail-in regime, and banking union will establish a Single Resolution Mechanism (SRM) for the Eurozone. Progress in other jurisdictions has been slower, but can be anticipated to accelerate, now that the EU has enacted its legislation.

Table 4.1 Resolution Regimes: Implementation of FSB Key Attributes

Jurisdiction	Scope	Resolution Authority	Resolution Powers	Contract clarity	Creditor safeguards	Resolution funding	Cross-border	Resolvability assessment	RRPs	Info sharing
G-SIB home										
United States		✓	✓	✓	✓	✓		✓	✓	✓
EU		✓	✓	✓	✓	✓	✓	✓	✓	✓
Switzerland	✓	✓	✓	✓	✓		✓	✓	✓	✓
Japan	✓	✓	✓		✓	✓	✓	✓	✓	✓
China		✓			✓			✓	✓	
Other FSB members										
Hong Kong		✓	✓							
Singapore		✓	✓				✓	✓	✓	✓
Australia		✓	✓		✓					✓
India		✓								✓
Korea	✓	✓	✓					✓		✓
Indonesia		✓	✓					✓		✓
Canada		✓	✓	✓				✓		✓
Mexico		✓			✓					
Argentina		✓				✓		✓		
Brazil	✓	✓	✓							
South Africa		✓							✓	
Turkey	✓	✓	✓					✓		✓
Saudi Arabia	✓	✓	✓		✓			✓		✓
Russia	✓	✓	✓							✓

Source: FSB 2013i, EU 2013. Column headings refer to key attributes (see FSB 2013i for complete description).

Resolution regimes generally allocate to the supervisor the responsibility to "pull the trigger" (i.e., make the determination that the bank should enter resolution). The supervisor is empowered to do so, when the bank reaches the point of non-viability, that is, when the bank no longer meets threshold conditions and is unlikely to be able to do so in the near future. Thus, the resolution statutes generally discourage forbearance. Such prompt corrective action prevents the bank from gambling for resurrection, reduces the loss that creditors are likely to incur and raises the probability that bail-in of investor obligations will be sufficient to recapitalise the bank (see the next section "Triggering resolution").

Resolution regimes assign responsibility for stabilisation and restructuring to a resolution authority, in the same sense that an administrator or insolvency practitioner takes responsibility for a non-financial corporation upon the commencement of bankruptcy proceedings. Like an administrator, the resolution authority should be able to take decisions for the business, including without limitation selling assets, lines of business or even the bank as a whole.

The resolution authority should be a public body with operational independence, sound governance and transparent processes. It should have responsibility for implementing the resolution of the failed bank in line with the provisions of the resolution statute.

The resolution regime should set out the options that the resolution authority may use to resolve a failed bank, along with any procedures that the resolution authority must follow in order to utilise a specific resolution tool. Ideally, the resolution authority should have a number of tools at its disposal that it can use either singly or in combination with one another. Resolution tools options include (i) liquidation and pay-off of insured deposits; (ii) asset-transfer to a third party and/or to a bridge bank; (iii) deposit or insured deposit transfer to third party and/or to a bridge bank; (iv) sale of the business/bank as a whole to a third party;

(v) "bail-in" of liabilities issued by the bank and/or its parent holding company; and (vi) "temporary public ownership." To resolve a G-SIB it is particularly important that the resolution authority have the bail-in tool.

The resolution regimes should also set out the "intervention target," namely, the legal vehicle within the banking group to which the resolution tool shall be applied. Generally this is the operating bank, but some options may also involve intervention at the level of the bank's parent. This is particularly important for the so-called single point of entry (SPE) approach (see "Dealing with cross-border issues" later).

Options involving the use of public money will generally require prior approval of the finance ministry, and some options may require much more extensive prior consultation or approval. For example, in the United States, a so-called triple-key process must be employed to open the door to using the Orderly Liquidation Authority (Title II) to resolve a failing US banking organisation. In planning for resolution, authorities should take into account the time that it may take to get such approvals. If possible, the resolution authority should conduct any preliminary analysis as well as complete a draft recommendation to use the tool before or at the point at which the decision is taken to pull the trigger and put the bank into resolution. With such preparation, the decision to pull the trigger and the decision to use the tool can be taken immediately one after another or practically simultaneously so that the resolution authority can devote the bulk of the real time in the interval between pulling the trigger and the reopening of the markets on the next business day to the many tasks necessary to assure successful stabilization (see later).

The resolution regime should also set out the criteria that the resolution authority should use in choosing among the resolution tools. Ideally, the standard should be the maintenance of financial stability, and most resolution regimes do include a provision to this effect. However, most regimes restrict this consideration to the maintenance of financial stability in the home market. There is no explicit reference to global financial stability or to financial stability in foreign jurisdictions.

This is a serious shortcoming. If the home country focuses on or gives preference to the home market, either as a matter of domestic law or policy preference, foreign jurisdictions that are host to the branches, subsidiaries or affiliates of the home country bank may well feel compelled to take countervailing measures, such as requiring the banking group to ring fence its operations in the foreign jurisdiction. This will fragment financial markets and reduce efficiency without necessarily improving resolvability or assuring financial stability (see later).

The resolution regime should also set a framework for the resolution authority to work with other authorities, including the central bank, the deposit guarantee scheme and the supervisory authority. For resolution to succeed, the stabilised "bank-in-resolution" must have access to liquidity (see below). Given the large amounts that may be required, the unstable environment that is likely to prevail at the time such amounts are required and the extremely short time frame available, adequate liquidity is likely for all practical purposes to involve official sources and/or guarantees. The resolution regime should facilitate such liquidity provision.

Similarly, the resolution regime should assure that the resolution authority coordinates with the deposit guarantee scheme (DGS) so that each authority knows and executes its respective role in (i) determining the amount of insured deposits (in aggregate and if necessary by depositor), and (ii) communicating with depositors, with the bank's management and board and with the bank's supervisor.

In addition, the resolution regime should assure that the resolution authority coordinates with the supervisory authority of the bank-in-resolution as well as with the supervisory authorities of any FMIs in which the bank-in-resolution is a participant. This will facilitate the bank-in-resolution's ability to retain or renew the authorisations and memberships that it requires in order to resume customer operations at the start of the next business day (see later).

Finally, the resolution regime should set out standards to which the resolution authority should be held accountable as well as the rights of creditors during the resolution process. Specifically, the resolution regime should make clear which steps, if any, require prior approval or judicial review. As a practical matter, these should be kept to a minimum, if resolution is to be workable. As emphasised earlier, the time frame for resolution is quite short, if continuity of customer service is to be maintained. It is simply impractical to use large portions of that short interval in review procedures. For the resolution authority to stabilise the bank-in-resolution, it must be free to act quickly.

Most resolution regimes allow for this. They restrict pre-approval to a minimum, mandate that judicial review be conducted ex post and limit any claims by creditors of the bank to the difference between what they did receive and what they would have received, had the bank gone into liquidation ("no creditor worse off" principle).

If such a difference exists, creditors would have recourse not to the resolution authority, but potentially to a resolution fund financed by the industry, not the general taxpayer. The resolution regime should also set the basis for such a fund, including the purposes for which such a fund might be used, who should be liable for contributions to the fund, whether funding should be ex ante or ex post, how such a fund would interact with the deposit guarantee scheme and any bank levy, how such a fund should be structured and what claims, if any, does the resolution fund have on the estate of the failed bank.[4]

Triggering resolution

Resolution begins when the bank's supervisor "pulls the trigger." Generally, this involves a finding by the supervisor that the bank no longer fulfils threshold conditions or the minimum requirements for maintaining its license. This will generally be the case when the bank has exhausted its recovery options and has reached the point of non-viability, that is, the point at which it can no longer fund itself in private markets and has no reasonable prospect of being able to do so again in the near future.

In practical terms, running out of liquidity is likely to be the proximate signal that the bank has reached the point of non-viability, especially for G-SIBs that finance themselves extensively in wholesale markets. Accordingly, the central bank is likely to play a significant role in deciding when the trigger to resolution should be pulled.[5] If the central bank provides liquidity to the bank, the supervisor (particularly if it is the central bank) will generally be inclined to defer putting the bank into resolution. In contrast, if the central bank denies the bank access to its liquidity facilities, the supervisor (if it is not the central bank) has little choice but to put the bank into resolution. Indeed, without the concurrence of (and provision of liquidity by) the central bank, it is difficult, if not impossible for the supervisor alone to exercise forbearance and allow the bank to remain in operation beyond the point of non-viability.[6]

That is all to the good, for the supervisor should avoid forbearance. Allowing the bank to continue in operation, possibly via the extension of emergency liquidity assistance, beyond the point of non-viability can induce the bank to "gamble for resurrection." With nothing left to lose, management and shareholders of the bank may attempt to restore its capital by investing in assets with extraordinarily high prospective returns. But such assets also generally carry higher risks, and losses are much more probable than gains. Simply delaying resolution is therefore much more likely to increase losses to creditors who remain than to restore the institution to health.[7] Prompt initiation of resolution is the key to preserving value for creditors (including depositors) and assuring continuity. Consequently, the supervisor should not pull the trigger too late.

Nor should the supervisor pull the trigger too early. In particular, the supervisor should avoid, if at all possible, pulling the trigger before the end of the business day in the westernmost jurisdiction in which the bank does business. Putting a bank into resolution in the middle of the business day maximises the possible disruption to financial markets and financial market infrastructures.[8] So it makes sense to wait until the point in the 24-hour clock when markets actually close for a few hours. This is generally the end of the business day in the United States.

Ideally, the supervisor should initiate resolution at the close of business on a Friday. This gives the authorities and financial market participants some 36–48 hours in real time from the closing in North America on Friday to the opening in Asia on Monday to put in place the measures necessary to stabilise the institution so that it can meet the continuity requirement and reopen for business on Monday. These measures are considerable in number and complexity, particularly for a globally systemically important bank, and it is advantageous to take the extra time that a weekend affords rather than attempt to do everything literally overnight.

Stabilising the bank-in-resolution

Once the supervisor has pulled the trigger, the resolution process moves on to its next and most critical phase: stabilisation. In the case of a bank, this means above all five things: (i) recapitalising the failed bank; (ii) assuring that the bank has adequate liquidity when it reopens for business; (iii) assuring that the bank retains or renews all relevant authorisations in the jurisdictions in which it does business; (iv) assuring that the bank retains access to relevant financial market infrastructures; and (v) the authorities' communicating effectively with each other, with depositors, creditors and investors of the failed bank and with the public at large.

Stabilising the bank-in-resolution also means overcoming certain obstacles. These include the rights of certain enti-ties, such as derivatives counterparties and repo providers, to terminate their contracts upon "default" by the bank, to demand immediate repayment by the bank of any obligation due and to obtain such immediate repayment via the sale of any collateral that the bank had provided. Failure to deal with this obstacle can scupper what might otherwise have been a successful stabilisation.

Finally, in the case of a G-SIB stabilisation requires some form of international cooperation between the home resolu-tion authority and the host resolution authorities in the coun-tries in which the G-SIB has branches and/or subsidiaries.

Recapitalising the failed bank

The first step toward stabilising the bank-in-resolution is the most important. This is to recapitalise the failed bank. Without such a recapitalisation, resolution will fail, at least for a G-SIB. That is likely to disrupt financial markets and damage the economy at large.

For resolution to succeed, recapitalisation of the failed bank must be done without recourse to public money. The finance ministry cannot simply write a cheque and subscribe to new equity in the bank. Resources for recapitalisation should come from investors, not taxpayers.

Theoretically, these investor resources could come from outside the failed bank, but as a practical matter they are unlikely to do so in the time frame required (see Box 4.1). For systemically important banks recapitalization of the bank is likely to succeed if and only if the resources for recapitalisa-tion are already in the bank. This will be the case if enough of the bank's liabilities can be "bailed-in," that is, written down or converted into equity of the bank. Bail-in can recapitalise the bank. This satisfies the necessary condition for the bank to continue in operation.

For bail-in to work effectively within the time frame relevant for preservation of continuity, a number of conditions have to hold: (i) the resolution authority has to have the statutory authority to implement bail-in immediately; (ii) bail-in has to respect the creditor hierarchy; (iii) bail-in of investor instruments should be sufficient to recapitalise the bank; and (iv) bail-in of investor instruments should not trigger cross-default clauses.

Box 4.1 Resolution through sale to a third party: unlikely to be a tool for G-SIBs

Certainly in the crisis there were a number of instances where the authorities sold a bank-in-resolution to a third party. But such episodes have not been uniformly successful. They pose what might be called contract risk to the acquirer and concentration risk to the taxpayer.

Contract risk stems from two sources, the compressed time frame available to conclude such deals and the ability of the authorities to unilaterally change the terms of such deals after the fact. The compressed time frame available to complete a deal means the acquirer has little or no time to conduct due diligence. As a result, the acquirer may underestimate the problems at the target bank and/or the difficulty it will face in assimilating and integrating the target bank with its own operations. Although the resolution authority can attempt to alleviate this problem by pre-marketing an institution that is in imminent danger of failing, such an exercise often confirms the depth of the troubled institution's problems and highlights the fact that it may be advantageous for the acquirer to wait until the "target" actually fails, for at that point the acquirer may be able to buy the bits it wants (and only the bits it wants) at a fire sale price.

A second source of contract risk stems from post-completion revision of the terms of the contract by the authorities. This may result in the acquirer's failing to receive expected tax rebates and/or the acquirer's being held liable for misconduct engaged in by the seller prior to the completion of the deal, even though the acquirer had explicitly agreed with the seller that such liabilities would remain the responsibility of the seller. Such revisions effectively cap or even eliminate the upside from making large acquisitions on extremely short notice, and will make institutions reluctant to bid, particularly if they do not have the opportunity to conduct due diligence.

In addition to the reluctance of potential acquirers to bid, public authorities may become less willing to sell a bank-in-resolution to a third party, particularly if the failed bank were a G-SIB. Quite aside from any financial support/taxpayer assistance that the resolution authority might be required to provide, such a deal would surely make a "too big to fail" bank into a "much, much too big to fail" bank. It would also very likely pose anti-trust or state-aid considerations.

Statutory authority to implement bail-in

Bail-in is an essential resolution tool, if losses are to be allocated to investors rather than borne by taxpayers. Accordingly, the resolution regime should

- *give the resolution authority the power to bail-in liabilities issued by the bank.* This so-called statutory bail-in should ideally be reinforced by contractual provisions in the instruments themselves as well as disclosure to investors that the instrument is subject to bail-in, if the bank enters resolution.

  Technically, there should be no limit on the liabilities subject to bail-in. Losses can potentially be imposed on any and all liabilities issued by the bank, including deposits (in the case of insured deposits such losses would be incurred by the deposit guarantee scheme rather than the depositor). As a practical matter, however, it will be useful for the statute as a matter of law or the resolution authority as a matter of regulation or policy to establish a pecking order for bail-in. This should conform to the creditor hierarchy (see later).

- *empower the resolution authority to implement bail-in immediately upon the bank's entry into resolution without prior judicial review.* Judicial review should be limited to ex post proceedings. Any claims of creditors for compensation should be limited to the amount that the creditor would have received had the bank been put into liquidation ("no creditor worse off" principle).

Bail-in should respect the creditor hierarchy

Giving the resolution authority the power to implement bail-in is just the start. How the authority does it matters just as much. As indicated earlier, bail-in should respect the creditor hierarchy. It should effectively work up the liability structure of the bank in reverse order of seniority, starting at Additional Tier 1 capital (e.g., preferred stock) and progressing to Tier 2 capital (e.g., subordinated debt). As these instruments count towards the bank's capital requirements, they are unquestionably investor obligations, not customer obligations. They should be subject to mandatory immediate bail-in upon the entry of the bank into resolution. Note that under Basel III this contractual provision must be fulfilled for Additional Tier 1 and Tier 2 capital instruments. If they are to continue to count as capital, such instruments must be subject to write-down or conversion at the point of non-viability.

If bail-in of these capital instruments is insufficient to recapitalise the bank, bail-in will have to proceed further up the liability structure. To the extent that bail-in has to do so, it is immensely helpful, if there is an additional class of investor obligations that is senior to subordinated debt but junior to customer obligations. Senior unsecured debt potentially fills this role, and largely does so where deposits have preference and derivatives are governed by netting contracts and margining agreements. In this case, senior debt effectively acts as a "mezzanine" layer of capital.

Conceptually, bail-in can proceed all the way up the liability structure, so that deposits and derivatives could potentially be bailed-in. But actually doing so is likely to prevent achievement of the continuity objective. So as a practical matter, attention needs to be paid to assuring that the bank has enough investor obligations outstanding to absorb even extreme losses. This will allow the resolution authority to recapitalise the bank whilst keeping customer obligations intact. That will promote continuity.

Bail-in of investor instruments should be sufficient to recapitalise the bank

For this reason, the authorities are contemplating imposing a "gone concern" or reserve capital requirement on banks.[9] This would require banks to maintain capital, such as preferred stock (Additional Tier 1) or subordinated debt (Tier 2) that could be subject to mandatory immediate bail-in, that is, written down or converted into CET1 capital upon the entry of the bank into resolution. Note that such write-down or conversion features are compulsory if the instrument is to count as capital under Basel III.

There is considerable discussion as to the amount of reserve capital that a bank should be required to issue, but a sensible starting point is that the reserve capital should be sufficient – once it is converted into CET1 capital – to allow the bank-in-resolution to meet minimum CET1 capital requirements. Such a requirement would effectively allow the bank to "reboot" or restart operations (and so preserve continuity) as long as the loss suffered by the bank was less than the CET1 capital that the bank held prior to the entry into resolution.

In addition to assuring that there is enough reserve capital to bail-in, care needs to be taken that the bail-in of investor instruments does not trigger cross-default of customer instruments, such as derivatives or repurchase agreements, such that counterparties to the bank-in-resolution could execute close out of derivative contracts and/or liquidation of collateral (see "Dealing with qualified financial contracts").

The bail-in process should mirror normal bankruptcy procedures

For bail-in to work, the process that the resolution authority will follow has to be clear to investors. Ideally, this process would follow normal bankruptcy practice as closely as possible. That requires the resolution process not only to respect the creditor hierarchy but also to establish the terms on which investor liabilities will be written off and/or converted into equity.

But these terms need not, indeed should not, be established during the stabilisation phase. They should either be set prior to the entry of the bank into resolution as part of the terms of the instrument or determined during the restructuring phase. For the pre-set instruments the resolution authority should commit to executing conversion or write-down in line with the terms of the instrument. For instruments without pre-set features that are subject to mandatory immediate bail-in, the resolution authority should be empowered to put a stay on payments to investor obligations (see Figure 4.2) and to establish, in coordination with creditors, the terms of write-off or conversion to equity during the restructuring phase.[10]

Resolution would therefore proceed as follows: When the bank reaches the point of non-viability, the supervisor declares that the bank fails to meet threshold conditions and puts the bank into resolution. The resolution authority immediately bails in the Additional Tier 1I capital, the Tier 2 capital and the senior debt subject to bail-in.[11] This expands the immediate loss-bearing capacity of the bank and effectively recapitalises it. In exchange for their original instruments, investors subject to mandatory bail-in obtain receivership certificates or proceeds notes that entitle them to the proceeds that the resolution authority may over time realise from restructuring the bank-in-resolution.[12] Such

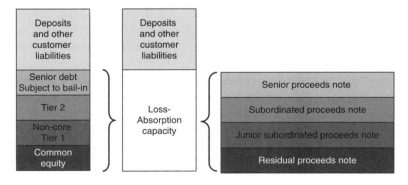

Figure 4.2   Bail-in via stay on investor capital

proceeds may result from the sale of assets, lines of business or the entire bank and/or from the earnings of the bank.

Any cash realised is distributed to the holders of the receivership certificates in accordance with strict seniority. Proceeds go first to holders of certificates (senior proceeds note) representing the claims of holders of senior debt subject to bail in. Once these claims have been fully satisfied, any remaining proceeds are distributed to more junior creditors, again according to strict seniority. To the extent that a creditor receives less than it would have done had the bank been liquidated, the creditor has a claim for compensation for the difference.[13]

Such an arrangement is sufficient to allow the resolution authority to recapitalise the bank-in-resolution during the stabilisation phase. This assures that the bank-in-resolution is solvent and allows it to proceed to the next step in the stabilisation process, namely, obtaining adequate liquidity (see later). The determination of the actual terms and conditions on which the investor obligations convert into equity can be deferred to the restructuring phase (see later).

Assuring the bank-in-resolution has adequate liquidity

Recapitalising the bank-in-resolution through bail-in of investor obligations is necessary but not sufficient to stabilise it. Continuity of operation can only be assured if the bank-in-resolution has access to adequate liquidity.

The liquidity demands on the bank-in-resolution could be very large indeed. Outflows from the bank are likely to increase very significantly. As soon as the bank-in-resolution opens for business on Monday, there is the very strong likelihood that any funds provider entitled to withdraw its money will do so. Additionally, inflows of cash into the bank-in-resolution are likely to decline dramatically. Where possible, clients of the bank-in-resolution will have changed their settlement instructions to stop their counterparties from paying in money to their accounts at the bank-in-resolution.

Consequently, for stabilisation to succeed, the bank-in-resolution must have lined up adequate sources of liquidity prior to reopening for business. Collateral is key. Once the bank has entered resolution, any provider of liquidity is likely to insist that this be done on a fully collateralised, super-senior basis in a manner analogous to the provision of debtor-in-possession financing in US Chapter 11 bankruptcy proceedings.

The framework for such a liquidity facility needs to be put in place well in advance of the bank being put into resolution. The framework should cover four factors:

1. The priority of the liquidity facility relative to other liabilities on the bank-in-resolution. As a practical matter, liquidity facilities to the bank-in-resolution will need to be on a super-senior basis so that they would have priority in liquidation over all unsecured creditors.
2. The pool of collateral backing the facility. As a practical matter this should be a charge over the unencumbered assets of the bank-in-resolution, including without limitation the investments of the parent bank in its subsidiaries. Any proceeds from asset sales should go towards repaying the facility.
3. The allocation of loss, should the bank-in-resolution fail to repay the facility, and the liquidation of the collateral prove insufficient to repay the facility.
4. How and where the bank-in-resolution might draw on such a liquidity facility.

To facilitate the possible arrangement of liquidity to a bank-in-resolution, it would make sense for the authorities to require banks whilst healthy to:

- *assure that they can seamlessly transfer collateral pledged to one lender (e.g., repo provider) to another.* Much of the demand for liquidity at the open of business on Monday will come from lenders who are secured, but who would prefer to avoid the possible complications that could arise if the resolution process were to become disorderly. Repayment of such lenders should bring about the immediate return of the collateral pledged to such lenders.

This should be done on the basis of repayment versus release so that the bank-in-resolution regains control over the collateral pledged to the lender being repaid at the same time that the repayment occurs. This will facilitate the ability of the bank-in-resolution to pledge the returned collateral to the new liquidity provider.

- *keep track of their unencumbered assets and assure that they can be pledged as collateral.* To the extent that the bank-in-resolution has unencumbered assets, these can potentially serve as collateral for the liquidity provider, if the bank-in-resolution can provide documentation as to their amount. This will only be possible if the bank-in-resolution can retrieve such information from systems established well before the supervisor pulled the trigger to resolution, such as those that might be used to support the development of a so-called collateral budget (see Chapter 2 "Measuring liquidity risks").
- *put in place pledge agreements that could be activated if the bank were to enter resolution.* This will assure that the potential liquidity provider can rapidly obtain control over the collateral that the bank-in-resolution has available to pledge.
- *conduct periodic "fire drills" to test operational procedures required for rapid pledge of collateral to a liquidity provider.* If a bank does enter resolution, liquidity provision to the bank-in-resolution must function without a hitch. To assure that it does, if required to do so, it makes sense to rehearse the concrete steps that the bank-in-resolution would have to take to pledge assets to a liquidity provider. The bank may also wish to consider (and the supervisor may require) the bank to pre-position collateral with the central bank, especially during the recovery phase (possible run up to resolution).

These steps are the minimum that can and should be done whilst the bank is healthy so that liquidity provision can proceed smoothly, if the bank does enter resolution. However, more could be done in advance, both to assure that the bank had unencumbered assets to serve as collateral as well as to set the terms and conditions on which a liquidity provider might extend credit to a bank-in-resolution.

From the standpoint of the bank-in-resolution, the greater the amount of unencumbered assets the bank has, the greater the potential funding the bank can obtain. One place to start is to assure that the bank restricts pledges of collateral to the trust for its covered bonds and securitization issues to the minimum required under the indentures to such instruments. But that may not be enough to assure that the bank has unencumbered assets to offer as security to a liquidity provider to the bank-in-resolution. Consequently, it may make sense to put limits on the encumbrance that a bank may incur whilst healthy so that it has some collateral in reserve, should it enter recovery or resolution.[14]

Finally, a word on documentation. As noted earlier, the first step is to assure that the liquidity provider can take a pledge over collateral assigned by the bank-in-resolution to the liquidity provider. As a practical matter, this has to be established well before the bank enters resolution. Ideally, the authorities should also indicate the terms of a draft framework agreement on which liquidity could be provided to the bank-in-resolution, if a decision were made to provide the facility. This would include covenants on the bank-in-resolution, such as (i) a requirement that any proceeds from the sale of assets should go toward paying down the facility; (ii) a prohibition on paying any dividends or making any distributions to the holders of proceeds notes (see earlier) until such time as the liquidity facility has been fully repaid with interest; and (iii) a prohibition on the bank's pledging unencumbered assets as collateral to third parties without a corresponding reduction in the outstanding liquidity facility or a waiver from the provider of the liquidity facility.

Note that such a draft framework agreement need not imply that the authorities themselves would provide liquidity to the bank-in-resolution. In particular, the central bank need not provide credit to any institution that it considers unviable, and the central bank should make clear that meeting the conditions set out in the framework agreement are a necessary but not sufficient condition for the central bank to provide credit to the bank-in-resolution.

However, setting out the terms of a framework agreement in advance is a step toward what might be called "constructive certainty" (see later). This has two advantages. First, it puts holders of the bank's investor obligations on notice that if the bank-in-resolution does obtain a liquidity facility, it will be on a collateralized basis and that the bank-in-resolution will have to fully repay the facility before it can make distributions or pay dividends to the holders of proceeds notes. That in turn should induce investors to demand information from the bank regarding the amount of its unencumbered assets as well as limit the pledge of such assets to the pools backing the bank's covered bonds and/or securitization issues.

Second, setting out the terms of the framework agreement may make it possible for private sector lenders to participate in the liquidity facility to the bank-in-resolution, for it outlines what the authorities are likely to permit the bank-in-resolution to do as well as the additional covenants that the lender would enjoy.

Assuring continued authorisation of the bank-in-resolution

In addition to recapitalising the bank-in-resolution and assuring that it has adequate liquidity, the resolution authority will need to assure that the bank-in-resolution retains its authorisation to act as a bank. In other words, the entry of the bank into resolution should not result in the revocation of the bank's license and a requirement for the bank-in-resolution to reapply for a license. Instead, a process should be in place to treat the entry into resolution as a change in control process, with control passing from the owner of the bank to the resolution authority and pre-approval of the resolution authority as "fit and proper" to run the bank-in-resolution. This will generally be the case for domestic banks or institutions headquartered in the banking group's home country, but may give rise to issues for internationally active groups (see "Dealing with cross-border issues").

Assuring continued access to financial market infrastructures

The resolution authority should also assure that the bank-in-resolution continues to have access to FMIs, such as payment systems, securities settlement systems and central counterparties. If the bank-in-resolution is to function normally upon reopening for business on Monday, it will certainly need access to FMIs. Otherwise, it will not be able to make or receive payments, settle securities transactions or conduct derivative transactions.

To assure that continuity is in fact preserved, the resolution regimes for banks should be coordinated with those for the FMIs (see Figure 4.3). In particular, the FMI should not be allowed to exclude a bank from the FMI solely on the basis that the bank has gone into resolution. Unless the bank-in-resolution has actually failed to make a cash payment to the FMI when due, the FMI should delay excluding the bank-in-resolution from the FMI as well as delay initiating loss allocation mechanisms within the FMI (the "waterfall") for a period to allow the resolution authority to indicate that it has (a) recapitalised the bank and (b) assured adequate liquidity for the bank. With such assurance the FMI can keep in force the membership of the bank in the FMI. That will not only facilitate the resolution of the failed bank, but help assure that the FMI remains robust.[15]

Assuring effective communication

Last but by no means least, the resolution authority has to assure that communication is effective: between the

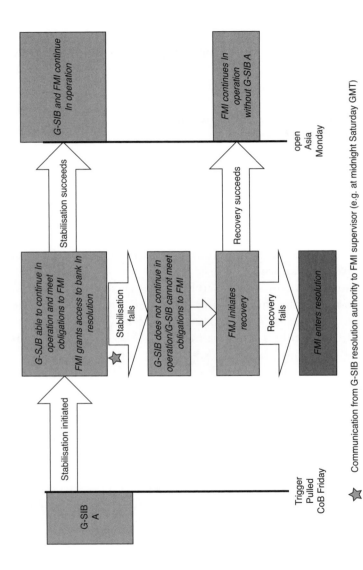

Figure 4.3   Coordination can create continuity

bank-in-resolution and the authorities; between the bank-in-resolution and its clients and counterparties; between the bank-in-resolution and the FMIs to which it belongs as well as among the authorities. Above all, communications to the market and to the public need to be frequent, straightforward and clear and to utilise all available media (e.g., television, radio, print and internet) in a coordinated fashion. However, communication also has to strike a delicate balance between the need to keep material matters confidential until the authorities have reached a decision with the requirement to disclose broadly to all investors the instant a decision has been reached.

Communication in crisis is easier if the resolution framework is clearly understood, not only by responsible officials, but also by key journalists across all media types. That allows officials to present steps, such as putting the bank into resolution, in their broader policy context and to explain how the resolution process will preserve continuity of customer functions at the failed institution as well as maintain stability in financial markets and the economy at large.

Restructuring the bank-in-resolution

Stabilising the bank-in-resolution is the first and most important step toward assuring that the failure of the bank will not significantly disrupt financial markets or the economy at large. But stabilisation is not the end of the story. The resolution authority must also decide what the future course of the bank-in-resolution should be.

In all likelihood, it will make sense for the resolution authority to act quickly. Even if the stabilisation has been successful, the resulting bank may be brittle. At least initially, the bank-in-resolution is unlikely to have a significant layer of reserve capital (e.g., subordinated debt), as this will have been converted into CET1 capital in the stabilisation phase. If new losses were to occur, customer obligations at the bank might be at risk if the losses ate through the newly created (as a result of the bail-in) CET1 capital. Consequently, customers may shift their business away from the bank-in-resolution, and the bank's key employees may depart. If this were to occur, the franchise value of the bank-in-resolution could quickly erode.

For this reason, the resolution authority may need to move quickly to sell assets, lines of business or even the firm as a whole to third parties who have the capital strength and funding necessary to sustain the business on an ongoing basis. Indeed, as part of its resolution planning the resolution authority should form an idea of the assets that it could sell and to whom, with the most logical candidates for rapid sale perhaps being transactions involving the assets and/or businesses that the bank may have identified in the recovery phase but failed to complete.

For those assets and businesses that the bank-in-resolution decides to keep (or cannot sell), the most pressing problem is likely to be liquidity – how can the bank-in-resolution fund the assets that remain on its books? Without funding, liquidation is practically the only choice open to the resolution authority. With funding, the resolution authority has the opportunity to conduct restructuring in a more orderly, but nonetheless rapid manner.

Rights of creditors during the restructuring phase

The goal of the resolution authority in the restructuring phase is to work itself out of a job: either to sell the bank to a third party, to return the bank to the private sector or to wind the bank down. Strengthening the rights of creditors can accelerate that process and help assure that creditors are in fact no worse off than they would have been under liquidation.

In economic terms, the creditors are collectively the owners of the bank-in-resolution. They have a claim (in order of seniority) on the cash flows that the bank-in-resolution may generate, once any official liquidity facility is repaid. But the creditors do not have primary decision rights over the restructuring process. This rests with the resolution authority, and the resolution authority need not seek approval of its resolution plan from the bank or its creditors.

In general, resolution regimes provide that creditors should be no worse off than they would have been under liquidation, and some regimes mandate that creditors have recourse to a resolution fund for any deficiency that they might suffer. To limit the possible amount of such claims and to induce creditors to play an active and constructive role in the restructuring process it may therefore make sense to accord creditors some of the same rights that they would ordinarily enjoy in a bankruptcy proceeding for a non-financial corporation, particularly in the case where the bail-in of investor obligations has recapitalised the bank. Such rights might include:

- The right of first refusal with respect to any significant sale of assets, line of business, material subsidiary or the firm as a whole. This would serve as a check on the resolution authority's selling such assets or entities at a fire sale price to the detriment of the creditors. This right would be exercised by class of creditor starting with the most senior and progressing to more junior categories, finishing with common equity.
- The right to use receivership certificates as the means of payment in connection with disposals by the bank-in-resolution either in connection with an original bid or in exercising their right of first refusal. Effectively, creditors could offer to exchange their claims on the estate of the bank-in-resolution for some portion of the bank's assets or business.
- The right of a junior class of creditors to buy out the next most senior class of creditors at par plus accrued interest. Such an offer satisfies the claim of the more senior class in full and allocates to the more junior class the ownership rights that the more senior class might have obtained.

- the right of a creditor class to present a plan for reorganisation of the bank-in-resolution (formation of Newco) that would
  - provide for repayment in full of any official liquidity facility granted to the bank-in-resolution;
  - assure that Newco meets capital and liquidity requirements, including any requirement for reserve capital;
  - assure that the management and directors of Newco were fit and proper;
  - provide evidence that Newco has a sound, sustainable business model; and
  - have the concurrence of other classes of creditors.

In sum, such a reorganisation plan should demonstrate that Newco meets threshold conditions. To the extent that such a plan involves the infusion of additional cash (e.g., to fund the issuance of additional capital instruments and/or to serve as a cash alternative to any exchange offer that might be made), the plan should be fully and unconditionally underwritten.

As such rights would accrue to creditors as a class, banking organisations as well as resolution authorities may find it advantageous to put in place a mechanism to allow creditors to function as a class. Ideally, such a mechanism would be put in place whilst the bank is healthy so that it could function immediately upon the entry of the bank into resolution. The mechanism would include:

- a registry of the owners of the instruments in the class;
- a process to allow for transfers of ownership of the instruments in the class. Voting rights for matters affecting the class should be linked to the ownership of the instrument;
- a process to notify such owners of material information pertaining to the class, including any voting materials;
- an accelerated voting process;
- cram-down provisions. Approval by a supermajority (e.g., 90 per cent) of the votes in a class shall bind the class; and
- a standing creditors' committee to represent the interests of the class vis-à-vis other classes and the resolution authority. Prior to

the entry of the bank into resolution, the main function of this standing creditors' committee would be to monitor the covenants that the instrument might contain and to exercise any rights that the creditors might have under such covenants.

From a public policy point of view such a mechanism would enhance market discipline. In particular, it would reinforce to creditors that they were at risk if the bank entered resolution. They would be bailed-in, not bailed-out. From a creditor point of view, such a mechanism (particularly the standing creditors' committee) would facilitate monitoring (and so reduce the risk that the bank would enter resolution) as well as help reduce loss given resolution.

Overcoming barriers to resolution

Conceptually, the resolution framework outlined earlier (trigger, stabilisation and restructuring) works so that a bank can be resolved without cost to the taxpayer and without significant disruption to financial markets or the economy at large. As a practical matter, however, certain obstacles to resolution need to be overcome. These include dealing with qualified financial contracts, assuring the separation between investor and customer obligations and dealing with cross-border issues.

Dealing with qualified financial contracts

Certain obligations, known as qualified financial contracts, may pose a barrier to resolution.[16] Upon an event of default, the claim becomes immediately due and payable (it is exempt from the stay on payments to creditors). If the claim is not repaid, the holder of such obligations has the right to liquidate any collateral that the bank may have pledged to it and to keep the proceeds of such sale in satisfaction of the obligation. If the proceeds of the sale are insufficient to repay the obligation, the holder has an unsecured claim on the bank in default for the difference. If the proceeds of the sale are greater than the amount of the obligation, the holder returns the excess to the bank in default.

The two principal types of qualified financial contracts are repurchase agreements and derivative contracts. Together these instruments account for a significant share of a bank's balance sheet, particularly for banks with heavy involvement in trading activities. Under a repurchase agreement the lender buys securities from the borrower, who enters into a commitment to repurchase at the maturity of the agreement the securities at a fixed (and somewhat higher) price than the lender originally paid to the borrower. This difference in price is the economic equivalent of interest on a loan.

The securities transferred to the lender by the borrower are the economic equivalent of collateral. The price paid by the lender for the securities is at a discount or "haircut" to market value. This haircut serves to protect the lender against loss in the event that the borrower fails to repurchase the securities at the agreed price upon maturity. In effect, the haircut protects the lender against a possible fall in the price of the securities purchased from the borrower (see Chapter 2).

The obstacle to resolution stems from the fact that the lender has the right to sell the securities upon an event of default by the borrower. When selling the securities, the lender is primarily interested in getting a price sufficient to repay the loan with interest. Beyond that point any proceeds belong to the borrower. As a result, the lender may be inclined to accept offers for the securities that effectively give up much if not all of the haircut that the lender accepted when selling the securities.

The loss of the haircut has two effects – first, it increases the loss that the bank-in-resolution has to incur and increases the probability that bail-in will have to extend beyond investor obligations to unsecured customer obligations such as deposits. That would compromise continuity. Second, the sale of the securities pledged under repurchase agreements is a source of contagion from the bank-in-resolution to financial markets and potentially to the economy as a whole. If the sale results in the loss of the haircut, it may imply a decline in the market price and a fall in income and capital at all the institutions in the market that hold such securities in their trading (mark-to-market) book. This effect is amplified, if the securities sold serve as a reference in the valuation of Level 2 or Level 3 assets. Hence, the sale of securities pledged by the bank-in-resolution can pose significant problems for the market as a whole.

Similar problems arise in connection with derivative contracts. Under netting agreements, the counterparty to the bank-in-resolution can terminate the derivative contracts that it has with the bank-in-resolution. Upon termination the non-defaulting counterparty (NDC) calculates a close-out amount that the bank-in-resolution would owe under the netting contract. In making this calculation, the NDC is allowed to use its replacement cost. In other words, the NDC makes the calculation not at the mid-market rate that the bank-in-resolution had used to value its contracts but at the end of the bid-offer spread that favours the NDC. This increases the amount due to the NDC, and this large(r) amount becomes immediately due and payable upon an event of default by the bank-in-resolution.

Under margining agreements the bank-in-resolution may have pledged collateral to the NDC as security that it would in fact be able to pay the amount due the NDC, if close out were invoked. Under the terms of the derivative contract, the NDC has the same rights as the lender under a repurchase agreement to sell the collateral in satisfaction of its claims and to keep the proceeds. Accordingly, the same issues arise in connection with collateral pledged in connection with derivative contracts as those related to repurchase agreements (see earlier).

To avoid these problems, resolution regimes envision placing a stay on the ability of lenders under repurchase agreements and counterparties to derivative contracts to exercise their rights of termination. The purpose of the stay is to allow the resolution authority to arrange for the bank-in-resolution to be in the position to meet its obligations under the contracts. Either the bank-in-resolution is recapitalised via bail-in, or the resolution authority transfers the contracts to a bridge bank that will continue in operation.

This is at best a partial solution. The stay may not be enforceable in foreign jurisdictions or for transactions concluded under foreign law. Relying solely on a stay also leaves open the possibility that the lenders and/or counterparties would elect to terminate as soon as the stay expires. What is needed is a mechanism that assures that they will not. Nor does the stay alone cure the complications that arise, if a bank's parent holding company has guaranteed the performance of the bank subsidiary under such contracts. In such cases, the entry of the parent holding company into resolution or bankruptcy can trigger termination of repurchase agreements and/or derivative contracts under the cross-default provisions usually found in such contracts. This gives rise to the adverse effects described earlier and may obviate the so-called single point of entry approach to resolution (see later).

Perhaps the simplest way to overcome the barriers to resolution posed by qualified financial contracts is to exclude the entry into resolution as an event of default and to limit the right to terminate to the actual failure by the bank-in-resolution to meet a cash obligation due in full and on time. In any event, steps should be taken to eliminate the ability to terminate contracts at the bank level unless there is a default at that level. The entry of a parent holding company into resolution or bankruptcy should not trigger cross-default provisions in qualified financial contracts at the bank level.

Assuring the separation between investor and customer obligations

As stressed earlier, resolvability hinges on the ability to separate investor and customer obligations, so that losses can be imposed on the former but not the latter. That is essential in order to assure continuity and to eliminate the rationale for taxpayer support.

Such separation can be achieved if the liabilities of the bank are structured in a manner akin to that of a securitisation vehicle (see Figure 4.4), so that losses are incurred according to a "waterfall," starting with common equity and progressing through Additional Tier 1 capital and then Tier 2 capital. Resolvability is enhanced if there exists a mezzanine (senior) layer that would be senior to Tier 2 capital, but junior to deposits and other customer obligations. Such customer obligations would effectively become super-senior, and in many jurisdictions are effectively so, thanks to depositor preference and/or collaterallisation (e.g., covered bonds, derivatives under margining agreements, repos). The key to resolvability is having enough capital in reserve (second loss and mezzanine in the description given) that is available

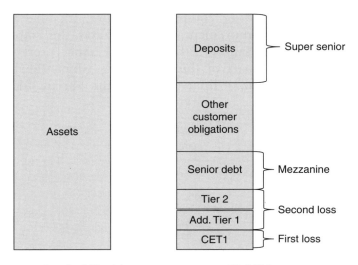

Figure 4.4   Resolvability hinges on structure of liabilities

to bear loss in the event that the bank reaches the point of non-viability and enters resolution.

Although it is technically possible to accomplish such a separation with the bank as the parent company,[17] structuring the operating bank as a subsidiary of a parent holding company (see Figure 4.5) makes the separation much clearer, particularly if reinforced by (i) a requirement that the parent invest in a minimum amount of subordinated debt issued by the bank subsidiary; and (ii) a prohibition on the parent holding company's engaging directly in operating activities.

The investment requirement assures that the bank has an amount of reserve capital outstanding that could be converted into CET1 capital, if the bank were to enter resolution. If the amount of reserve capital were greater than or equal to the minimum CET1 capital requirement (7 per cent of RWAs including the capital conservation buffer), the bail-in of the reserve capital at the bank level would be sufficient to recapitalise the bank, even if the loss wiped out the entire amount of CET1 capital that the bank had had prior to the entry into resolution.

The parent holding company structure, together with the investment requirement, also facilitates the stabilisation of the bank. Bail-in in the event the bank enters resolution should be part of the contract by which the bank subsidiary issues subordinated debt to the parent. Ideally,

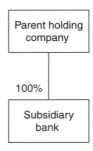

Figure 4.5   A resolvable banking structure

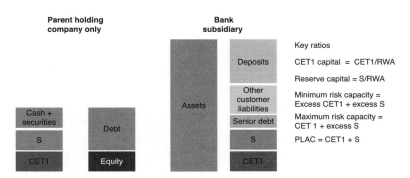

CET 1 = Common equity Tier 1 capital in the bank subsidiary
S = Subordinated debt in the bank subsidiary

Figure 4.6   Balance sheet overview

these contractual provisions would be reinforced by statute, but the contractual provisions alone should be sufficient to assure that bail-in could take place immediately upon the entry of the bank into resolution.

The investment requirement also helps solve the question of the rate at which the subordinated debt at the bank level should convert into CET1 capital. As the parent holding company owns both the debt and the equity, the bail-in does not dilute the parent's interest in the bank subsidiary: it continues to own 100 per cent of the bank subsidiary before and after the bail-in (provided the loss is less than the amount of the bank's primary loss-absorbing capacity [CET1 capital plus reserve capital]). Consequently, the bail-in can be accomplished either by the parent's structuring the sub-debt as a write-off bond (so that the profit from doing so accrues to the equity in the bank) or by the subsidiary bank converting the sub-debt into equity.

The parent holding company structure also facilitates the restructuring of the bank. Indeed, for losses less than the bank's Primary Loss Absorbing Capacity, the subsidiary bank remains solvent and the parent holding company (or the estate of the parent holding company, if the parent

holding company enters bankruptcy proceedings [see later])
will remain the owner of the subsidiary bank. There will not
be a change in control of the bank (as there would be if the
bank itself were the parent company and the subordinated
debt held by third-party creditors were bailed- in).

Note that the write-down of the parent's equity in the bank
subsidiary may force the parent holding company into bankruptcy, especially if the subsidiary bank-in-resolution cannot
pay dividends or interest to the parent. However, given the
simple structure of the parent holding company, such a bankruptcy proceeding at the parent only should be a straightforward matter, especially if handled in a manner similar to the
so- called Chapter 14 approach that has been proposed as an
amendment to the US bankruptcy code.[18] This would essentially transfer all the parent holding company's assets into a
new "bridge" holding company (Newco) financed entirely by
equity. This would become a going concern. The estate of
the original (and now bankrupt) parent holding company
(Oldco) would be entitled to any cash proceeds generated
by Newco (either via dividends or via the sale of assets) and
would distribute these to the creditors of Oldco in order of
strict seniority (see Figure 4.7).

The bankruptcy of the parent should not affect the subsidiary
bank-in-resolution, particularly if the proceeding entails a rapid
transfer of the parent's assets into a bridge holding company
that is 100 per cent equity financed. The immediate owner of
the bank (the bridge holding company) would remain solvent
until the last penny of the company's assets was written off.

However, this statement will not hold if the original
holding company had given a guarantee of the subsidiary
bank's obligations to third parties, so that the bankruptcy or
entry into resolution of the parent holding company triggers
cross-default at the bank subsidiary and gives counterparties
the right to terminate the derivative contracts that they had
concluded with the bank subsidiary. For this reason, resolution regimes envision imposing a stay on counterparties

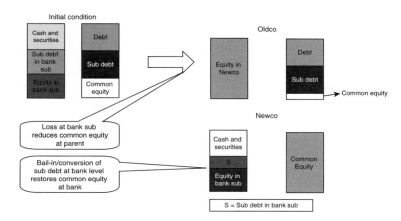

Figure 4.7 Bankruptcy of parent

being able to exercise their termination rights (see earlier). Ideally, this would be supplemented by a prohibition on the holding company's giving such guarantees, or, at a minimum, by eliminating the bankruptcy of the holding company as an event of default in the derivatives contracts concluded by the bank subsidiary.

Dealing with cross-border issues

Finally, resolution of a globally systemically important bank must tackle cross-border issues. G-SIBs are present via branches and subsidiaries in up to 100 or more different jurisdictions. Sorting out responsibilities of home and host authorities in advance is therefore critical, if the institution is to be resolvable. The principal areas to clarify are (i) resolution of a bank with foreign branches, (ii) the overall approach to resolution and (iii) the provision of liquidity to the bank-in-resolution.

Resolution of a bank with foreign branches: a question of principle

"Unitary" or "territorial"? Which principle should resolution authorities follow if a bank with foreign branches enters resolution?

The answer is clear: the unitary principle. Under this principle, all branches, domestic and foreign, are integral parts of the bank as a whole. There is a single resolution process, run by the home country resolution authority (see Figure 4.8). This allows the home resolution authority the opportunity to stabilise the bank, ideally through the bail-in of investor instruments and the provision of a liquidity facility (see later). That in turn allows the resolution authority time to restructure, sell or wind down the bank-in-resolution without having to liquidate assets at fire sale prices. This facilitates continuity, reduces losses to the estate of the bank-in-resolution and limits contagion to other participants in financial markets.

It is essential that both the host and the home country resolution authority accept and follow this principle. The host (foreign) jurisdiction needs to acknowledge that the branch in its jurisdiction is part of the home country bank and that the home country resolution authority will run the resolution process for the entire bank. In this case the foreign jurisdiction pools the assets of the foreign branch with the assets of the rest of the bank and the liabilities of the foreign branch

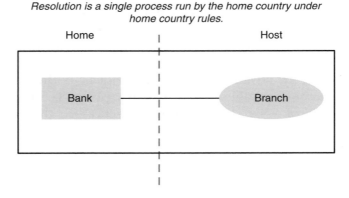

Figure 4.8 Bank with foreign branch: resolution under unitary approach

are paid in accordance with the rules of the home country. Effectively the foreign jurisdiction recognises the lead of the home country supervisor and home country resolution authority and accepts the decisions of the home country authorities including without limitation the transfer of the subsidiary bank's license to the bridge holding company in the event that the parent holding company enters bankruptcy proceedings.

The home country resolution authority also needs to follow the unitary principle. This involves an acceptance that the liabilities of the foreign branches are on a par with those of the bank's head office and domestic branches. Note that this commitment is easier to sustain, if the bank has an ample amount of reserve capital that can be bailed-in in the event the bank enters resolution. Without such reserve capital in place, the home country resolution authority may elect or be directed to prefer the obligations of the bank's domestic branches over the bank's foreign branches. This is particularly likely to be the case if the unitary approach to resolution would result in severe losses to domestic depositors and/or punitive levies on domestic banks under the domestic deposit guarantee scheme.[19]

In contrast, the territorial approach (see Figure 4.9) is a liquidation approach. Under this approach the foreign jurisdiction resolves the foreign branch separately from the rest of the bank. It uses the assets of the foreign branch to meet the obligations of the foreign branch to the creditors of that branch. Should any proceeds remain after the branch has fully met its obligations to its creditors, this excess would be remitted to the estate of the parent bank. Should a deficiency remain, the creditors of the foreign branch would have an unsecured claim on the estate of the parent bank. In effect, the territorial approach turns the liabilities of the foreign branch into what amounts to a covered bond, where the coverage constitutes the assets of the foreign branch. For this reason, the territorial approach is frequently reinforced by

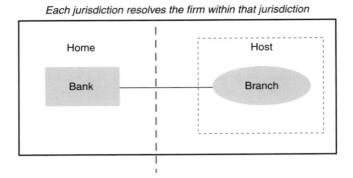

Figure 4.9   Resolution under a territorial approach

an asset maintenance requirement to assure that the foreign branch will have enough assets to cover its liabilities, if the bank enters resolution.

If the host country resolution authority follows the territorial principle and begins to liquidate the bank-in-resolution's branch in the host country, the home country may have to liquidate the parent bank as well. If it has to liquidate, that will stop continuity, increase losses to creditors and almost certainly disrupt financial markets and the economy at large. So the territorial approach amounts to something akin to a nuclear option.

Foreign authorities are particularly likely to want this option if the home country grants preference in resolution to creditors of the domestic offices of the bank, either generally or within a certain class of liabilities (e.g., deposits).[20] In such a case, the home country has the option to resolve the bank by transferring the obligations of the bank's domestic offices to a bridge bank along with the bank's best assets and leave the obligations of the bank's foreign branches (along with the bank's worst assets) behind in a rump bank. The bridge bank would continue in operation; the rump would not – it would be liquidated over time under the aegis of the home country resolution authority. As a result, creditors of the foreign branch would be likely to lose access to their funds for an extended period of time and to suffer severe losses as and when the estate of the rump bank made a distribution. The territorial approach of the foreign jurisdiction counteracts this by placing the liquidation of the foreign branch under the administration of the foreign resolution authority. And, the asset maintenance requirement effectively collateralizes the obligations of the foreign branch and therefore counteracts the preference that the home country seeks to give to creditors of the bank's domestic offices.

Unfortunately, there is not a universal acceptance that the unitary approach is the right principle to follow. A number of jurisdictions, notably including the United States, have the power to implement the territorial approach with respect to foreign banks, and some (again including the United States) have granted preference to domestic deposits.

Ideally, these countries would change their legislation to adopt the unitary approach, but one must realistically accept that this is unlikely to happen in the near future. However, what host country authorities can do is to commit the following:

- The host country authorities will refrain from initiating the resolution of the branch in the host country without giving prior notice to the home country authority and giving the home country authority the opportunity to
  - cure the deficiency in the branch; or
  - initiate resolution of the bank as a whole.
- If the home country authorities do initiate resolution of the bank as a whole, the host country authorities will refrain from initiating the territorial approach provided the home country authorities act to stabilise the bank-in-resolution via the bail-in of investor capital and the provision of liquidity facilities to the bank-in-resolution.

Such a commitment offers the best hope of avoiding the "mutually assured fragmentation" that would result if home and/or host authorities were to actually implement the territorial approach to resolving a globally systemically important bank.

The overall approach to resolution: the case for constructive certainty

The issue of how to deal with branches of an individual bank is a subset of the much more general issue, namely how home and host country resolution authorities should deal with a banking group that has many different subsidiaries in many different jurisdictions (see Figure 4.10). According to the FSB, the relevant authorities should develop an approach for each G-SIB and document this in a cooperation agreement.

Two approaches are under discussion. Under the first, single point of entry (SPE) approach, resolution is a unified, global process under the aegis of the home country resolution authority. Under the SPE approach, the failure of one or more subsidiaries to meet threshold conditions triggers resolution of the group as a whole. The home country resolution authority takes control of the parent holding company and acts to recapitalise the failing bank(s). This stabilises the banks in the group and the group as a whole

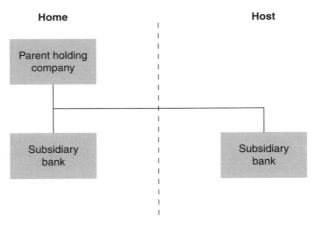

Figure 4.10   Banking group with domestic and foreign subsidiaries

serves as the basis for the provision of a liquidity facility (see later), so that "subsidiaries would remain open and continue operations."[21] The SPE approach therefore assures continuity and removes any need for the taxpayer to provide solvency support.

Under the second, multiple point of entry (MPE) approach, subsidiaries are resolved separately within each jurisdiction. If a subsidiary bank fails to meet threshold conditions, the resolution authority for that subsidiary resolves it, whilst the rest of the group continues in operation. In effect, the MPE approach follows the principle of limited liability and allows the parent holding company to walk away from a failing subsidiary.

Who should make the choice between the two approaches, and when should the choice be made? Should the choice be left entirely to resolution authorities, and entirely until resolution is initiated? That would be consistent with a long-standing bias among policymakers, particularly central banks, in favour of "constructive ambiguity." But this doctrine refers to the creation of doubt as to whether there will or will not be a bail-out.

What is required is "constructive certainty" – a method to assure that markets know that investors, not taxpayers, will bear the cost of bank failure. Although the authorities may prefer ambiguity, for it enables them to retain the option to decide based on the facts of a specific resolution case, more certainty as to the path the authorities would actually take is likely to enhance resolvability. Policymakers and firms need to map out in advance how an institution is likely to be resolved, and take steps – such as the institution-specific cooperation agreements advocated by the FSB – to anchor these commitments into what might be called a presumptive path. Not only will such a presumptive path underline that holders of investor obligations will indeed be exposed to loss, but it will enable investors in such instruments to form a better idea of the losses that they could incur, if resolution were required. That in turn will facilitate the sale of such instruments to investors and facilitate resolvability.

Today, no such certainty exists as to the presumptive path the authorities might follow. A firm can express a preference for resolution under an SPE approach, but there is no assurance that resolution authorities will respect or implement this choice. Alternatively, a firm can express a preference for an MPE approach, but there is no assurance that the resolution authorities will respect or implement this choice. There is a gap between theory and reality. In theory, all subsidiaries are equal. In practice, they are not. The bank subsidiary headquartered in the same jurisdiction as the parent holding company is plainly, in the eyes of the home country regulator, primes inter pares. This poses challenges to both the SPE and MPE approaches. Confronting those challenges holds the key to creating constructive certainty.

Single point of entry   The SPE approach is viable if and only if (i) the home country resolution authority is authorised, able and willing to assume command of what amounts to a global resolution syndicate; and (ii) the host countries are willing to accept such leadership by the home country resolution authority (see Figure 4.11).

For the SPE approach to work, the home country resolution statute must authorise the home country resolution authority to take control of the parent holding company upon (i) the failure of the group to meet threshold conditions on a consolidated basis, or (ii) in the event that a subsidiary bank fails to meet threshold conditions and is placed into resolution. However, seizing the parent due to losses at the subsidiary raises significant issues with respect to property rights, so that the authorisation to take control of the holding company may be (i) subject to prior approval by the central bank, finance ministry and/or head of government; (ii) restricted to certain resolution techniques, such as temporary public ownership, that involve the use of taxpayer

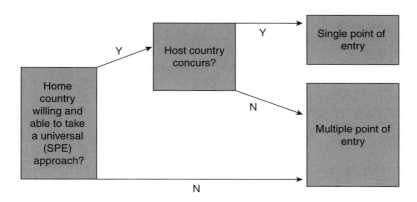

Figure 4.11 SPE approach requires concurrence of home and host

funds, and/or are restricted to cases where the failing bank is headquartered in the home country.[22]

From the standpoint of the host country authorities responsible for the home country's subsidiary in the host jurisdiction, this situation is not entirely satisfactory, as there is no guarantee the home country resolution authority can actually assume the role intended for it and assigned to it under the SPE approach. Not only does the home country resolution authority have to pass a test before it can implement the SPE approach, but the grades for that test are generally based on the impact that the failure of the G-SIB would have on financial stability in the home country only. Hence, from the vantage point of the host country authorities, it is unclear that the home country resolution authorities could always implement the SPE path, particularly if the losses prompting the entry into resolution were concentrated in the group's foreign subsidiaries.

For this reason, it will be entirely rational for host countries to require – if they are to concur with the SPE approach – some greater assurance that the home country will actually implement the SPE approach regardless of the source of the loss and that the SPE approach will actually result in the stabilisation of the subsidiary in the host country. Failing such reassurance, it is natural to expect host authorities to take measures to protect the creditors of the subsidiaries located within their jurisdiction.

Multiple point of entry   The central premise of the MPE approach is that resolution can take place at the level of each individual subsidiary according to the rules and procedures of that jurisdiction. For this to be the case, each of the subsidiaries should be self-sufficient, with separate funding and no inter-affiliate transactions. In particular, the bank subsidiaries should not invest in instruments issued by the parent holding company; should not hold cash balances with other entities within the group; and should refrain from using affiliates for services, such as cash management and/or custody that create a credit exposure to the affiliate. To the extent that the subsidiary obtains services from other affiliates within the group, the services should be provided from a separately capitalised central services subsidiary (rather than from another bank within the group) that can continue to provide services to the subsidiary in resolution for a transition period.

Under the MPE approach the premise is that the holding company can walk away from a subsidiary in country A where losses have exhausted its equity investment in that subsidiary. But the terms on which this could occur need to be spelled out. First, is each bank subsidiary within an MPE group required to issue an amount of reserve capital equal to the minimum CET1 requirement? This is the same requirement as the bank subsidiary has under the SPE approach. The only difference is the ability of the MPE bank to sell such debt to third parties. Second, to the extent that a bank within an MPE group does sell reserve capital instruments to third parties, is there a robust resolution process by which the holders of such instruments as a class can take control of the subsidiary bank-in-resolution? In particular, will the subsidiary bank be resolved on the unitary principle or the territorial principle (if the latter, the resolution process will in all likelihood result in liquidation rather than continuity; see earlier). Third, will all resolution authorities in the jurisdictions in which an MPE group does business confirm that they will not exercise what amounts to a "cross-resolution" provision, whereby country B takes the entry into resolution of the group's subsidiary in country A to put the group's subsidiary in country B into resolution and sell this subsidiary to a third party at a knock-down price?

Fourth, is the home country also willing to have the MPE process apply to the group's domestic bank so that the parent could keep healthy foreign subsidiaries whilst limiting its liability for losses at the domestic bank to the amount of its investment? It is doubtful that this would be the case, especially where the domestic bank is systemically important in the domestic market and legislation in the home country allows the resolution authority to take control of the parent holding company upon entry of the domestic bank into resolution. Even though the owners of the parent holding may conclude that it would be economically rational for them to walk away from the domestic bank, the economics for the home resolution authority point in the direction of exercising its option to take over the holding company, employ a single point of entry approach, provide a continuity guarantee to host countries with respect to the group's subsidiaries in the host country and use proceeds from the sale of the group's healthy foreign subsidiaries to reduce losses to creditors of the domestic subsidiary bank.

This brings us full circle. Although the SPE approach is likely to be most effective from a global standpoint in terms of preserving financial stability, political pressures in the home country (as well as the terms of the home country legislation) may lead to the impression that the home country wishes to have the option to implement an SPE approach when the losses have occurred at the domestic bank subsidiary, but reserve the right to resort to an MPE approach when the losses are at the foreign subsidiary. To defend against this possibility host countries will potentially want to ring fence their bank up front, demand significant infusions of capital up front and restrict inter-affiliate transactions.

Recent policy proposals by the United States illustrate the differing perspectives of home and host. As home, the United States advocates the SPE approach for US headquartered institutions and proposes that the FDIC act as a global resolution authority in a manner that will assure that subsidiaries "remain open and continue operations."[23] As host, the United States has expressed doubt regarding the ability of foreign banking organisations (FBOs) "to provide support to all parts of its organization." For this reason, the Federal Reserve Board, as the principal host regulator of FBOs in the United States, has imposed a rule requiring FBOs to establish intermediate holding companies that meet US standards. In the view of the Federal Reserve, this "reduces the need for an FBO to contribute additional capital and liquidity to its U.S. operations during times of home country or other international stresses, thereby reducing the likelihood that a banking organization that comes under stress in multiple jurisdictions will be required to choose which of its operations to support."[24]

Constructive certainty

Fragmentation is likely to be the end result of such conflict between home and host country objectives. Rather than assure G-SIBs can become global in death, jurisdictions are likely to attempt to force banks to become national in life, so that they can remain national in death. However, such fragmentation will diminish efficiency without necessarily improving resolvability. What is needed is a presumptive path – call it constructive certainty – that both home and host authorities can follow.

One possible approach is a hybrid between the SPE and MPE approaches (see Box 4.2). This would be driven by who holds the "reserve capital" that all bank subsidiaries would be required to issue: the parent holding company or third-party investors. It is based on putting and keeping a certain amount of strength (either from the parent holding company or third-party investors) up front into the subsidiary banks within a group, rather than requiring the parent holding company to act as a source of strength after the subsidiary bank has failed.

Box 4.2 A hybrid approach to resolution

For all groups designated as G-SIBs, this would entail the following steps:

1. Each bank subsidiary within a group to issue and keep outstanding "reserve capital" greater than or equal to the threshold level required for that bank under [3] or [4]. Such reserve capital shall be mandatorily convertible into CET1 capital in the bank immediately upon entry of the bank subsidiary into resolution.
2. The parent holding company may not pay dividends or make distributions unless all the group's bank subsidiaries – both domestic and foreign – meet both (i) their minimum CET1 capital requirement (7% of RWAs including the capital conservation buffer) and (ii) the "reserve capital requirement" outlined in [3] or [4].
3. *Where the parent holding company does not own 100% of the reserve capital issued by the bank subsidiary,*
   a. The threshold amount of reserve capital at the bank subsidiary shall be equal to the minimum required CET1 capital ratio (including capital conservation buffer) *plus* the SIFI surcharge. The terms and conditions for the conversion of such reserve capital into CET1 capital in the bank shall be established in advance, including the process by which the holders of such debt as a class could assume control of the subsidiary bank-in-resolution.[25]
   b. The bank subsidiary shall fulfil what might be called an "independence requirement" so that the bank subsidiary could continue in operation, even if the parent holding company and/or a sister affiliate were to enter resolution. This independence

---

requirement would include strict limits on inter-affiliate trans-actions. To the extent that the bank subsidiary obtained services from the rest of the group, contracts for such services should assure that such services could continue to be provided to the bank subsidiary for an extended transition period in the event that the bank subsidiary entered resolution, notwithstanding the possibility that such a subsidiary could cease to be part of the group.

4. *Where the parent holding company owns 100% of the reserve capital issued by the bank subsidiary,*

    a. The threshold amount of reserve capital at the bank subsidiary shall be equal to the minimum required CET1 capital ratio (i.e., 7%, including capital conservation buffer). The bank subsid-iary shall be prohibited from paying interest and dividends or making distributions to the parent holding company unless the subordinated debt issued to and held by the parent (the "reserve capital" ratio) exceeds the threshold amount. Should the bank subsidiary not be permitted to pay interest in cash to the parent holding, it shall pay interest in kind (i.e., it shall issue additional subordinated debt to the parent on the same terms and conditions as the previous debt in an amount equal to the interest payable).

    b. Should such PIK payments be insufficient to restore the reserve capital to the threshold 7% level, the subsidiary bank shall have the right to sell additional reserve capital to the parent holding company and the parent holding company shall have the obligation to subscribe to such capital. To help assure that the parent holding can meet such commitments, the parent holding shall maintain a reserve of cash and marketable securi-ties at the parent level equal to the SIFI surcharge for the group as a whole on a consolidated basis.

Together, the measures in the hybrid approach would assure that each of the group's bank subsidiaries – domestic or foreign – could be recapitalised in the event that the subsidiary in question failed to meet threshold conditions. Moreover, the measures in the hybrid approach go a long way to establishing a presumptive path for resolution. Finally, the measures should help assure host country authorities that the subsidiary in their country could be resolved without recourse to their taxpayer and without significant disruption to their economy.

The provision of liquidity to the bank-in-resolution

As outlined earlier for individual banks, recapitalisation is necessary but insufficient to stabilise the bank-in-resolution. In addition to fresh equity, the bank-in-resolution will need access to liquidity. This will be especially true for G-SIBs. If a G-SIB were to enter resolution, it would in all likelihood require very significant amounts of liquidity, starting immediately upon the opening of business in Asia.

The recapitalisation of the subsidiary banks via the conversion of reserve capital into CET1 capital should enable the bank-in-resolution to remain solvent and therefore to fulfil the minimum eligibility requirement to access liquidity from official sources (such as central banks) or private providers. Any such liquidity facility would be on a super-senior basis against the provision of collateral. For subsidiaries where third parties have supplied the bank's "reserve capital," the liquidity facility to that subsidiary would be based solely on that subsidiary's collateral as pledged to the "local" liquidity provider to that bank (such as that bank's resolution authority or central bank). In making this loan, the local liquidity provider would act as principal and keep the home country (group) resolution authority/central bank informed that it had made the loan. Should the subsidiary bank fail to repay the credit and the collateral prove insufficient to extinguish the bank's obligations to the local liquidity provider, the lender would have recourse against that subsidiary only and no claim on either the parent holding company or other subsidiaries within the group.

For the subsidiaries whose "reserve capital" is held by the parent ("integrated subsidiaries"), it would potentially be advantageous for the home country resolution authority to act as a global liquidity provider and arrange a global liquidity facility for the group's integrated subsidiaries as a whole. This would effectively allow collateral to be pooled across the group and funds to flow to the point at which they were most needed within the group's integrated subsidiaries. In practical terms, such a global liquidity provider would take a fixed and floating charge over the parent holding company's assets as well as over any unencumbered assets that the integrated subsidiaries might currently have or obtain in the future. To the extent that an integrated subsidiary's local resolution authority or central bank figured in such a facility, it would be as agents of the home resolution authority/central bank.[26]

Summary assessment

In sum, resolving a G-SIB is a complex, multi-faceted task. But it is a do-able task, on which banks and the authorities have already made much progress. What remains to be done are above all four things:

- Complete the reserve capital/bail-in regime so that banks can be readily recapitalised
- Complete arrangements for provision of liquidity to the bank-in-resolution
- Assure that resolution is not derailed either by derivatives counterparties or financial market infrastructures
- Conclude cooperation agreements among the G-SIB's supervisors and resolution authorities that create "constructive certainty" as to how the G-SIB would be resolved.

This would not only make banks resolvable, but it would also make customer obligations (e.g., deposits, derivatives) at the bank level approach the AAAA standard that customers ideally want (see Figure 4.12).[27]

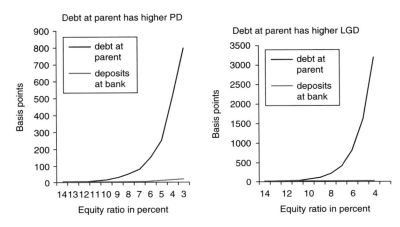

Figure 4.12   Structural subordination makes deposits significantly safer than parent company debt

5

Setting Up for Success

Together, the initiatives to make banks both less likely to fail and safe to fail will have a significant impact on banks, especially the G-SIBs that are at the heart of the global financial system.

Reform of regulation (see Chapter 2), supervision (see Chapter 3) and resolution (see Chapter 4) will change the environment in which banks must operate. Banks will have to comply with the rules if they are to survive. But to thrive, banks will also have to make the right choices – about the targets they aim to meet; about the business models they employ; about the markets in which they stay, enter or leave; and about developing the capabilities they will need in order to win. In short, banks have to set themselves up for success.

Regulation offers banks the opportunity to do so. In order to comply with regulatory and supervisory standards banks will have to spend vast amounts of money and time over the coming years to revamp their technology, their data and their systems and procedures. Banks that view these requirements simply as added cost will wind up with just that, added cost. Banks that recognise that much of the new regulation represents sound business practice can potentially make this spending do double duty. They can use the spending to improve their business model as well as comply with regulation. Those banks which do so will have significantly better prospects for success in the new environment.

Regulation and supervision establish the framework in which banks must operate

In broad terms, regulation and supervision establish (i) the boundaries within which a bank must choose its strategy, and (ii) the guidelines that banks must follow in implementing that strategy.

Regulation will frame the activities in which banks may engage, the structure banks may have, the capital that banks must keep, the liquidity that banks must maintain, the governance that banks must employ, the conduct banks must exhibit and the customers banks may serve. Supervisors will not only enforce these regulations, but seek to cut off the bank's ability to conduct a high-risk strategy.

Resolution reform will assure that market discipline reinforces supervisory discipline. Resolution reform will assure that investors, not taxpayers, will bear the cost of bank failure. Bail-in will replace bail-out. Consequently, investors will demand higher premiums to fund banking groups that take higher risk.

The boundaries set by regulation and resolution limit the risk a bank can pose, not only to depositors and the economy at large, but to some extent to investors. Although banks may complain that the guidelines are overly prescriptive, much of the guidelines in fact reflect good business practice. And if supervision is done well, investors as well as depositors and the economy at large will benefit.

Setting the overall risk boundary

In finance terms, regulators and supervisors are seeking to force banks into assuming lower risk. Resolution reform aims to eliminate the ratings pickup that banks derive from implicit government support so that there is no difference between a bank's stand-alone rating and its overall rating. Through tougher capital and liquidity requirements and more pro-active supervision, authorities are aiming to assure that banks maintain a stand-alone rating that is comfortably investment grade at all times (even at the trough of the cycle) so that the bank will remain a considerable distance from resolution (see Figure 5.1).

Guidelines are generally good business practice

In addition to setting boundaries on the overall risk a bank can take, regulation and supervision set guidelines on how a bank should conduct its business. Much, if not all, of these guidelines simply represents good business practice.

That is certainly the case for the overall thrust of regulation and supervision. To be successful, the bank must maintain adequate capital and liquidity. To do so, it should have good governance, good risk management, good contingency planning and so on. Although banks may rightly quibble with the merits of particular regulations and/or supervisory procedures (see Chapter 2), the overall intent and direction of regulation and supervision is to assure that banks are well managed.

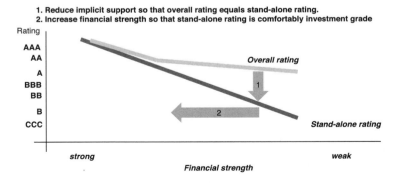

Figure 5.1   Supervisory strategy to reduce risk

Supervision can add value

In fact, supervision can add value. As highlighted in the Introduction, prudential regulation is akin to the covenants that a lender or guarantor would impose upon a borrower; and supervision is akin to the monitoring that the lender would undertake to assure that the borrower adhered to the covenants. And the "minding" that a supervisor conducts is similar – if done well – to the discipline that a private mezzanine capital fund would impose on its investee companies, if they were to exhibit weakness.[1]

This will become increasingly apparent and important to investors in bank or holding company obligations subject to bail-in, for they will be exposed to loss under the reforms to resolution under way in key jurisdictions. If resolution really does impose losses on such instruments to loss, actual and prospective investors will have an interest in assuring that supervision:

- monitors banks accurately;
- "minds" firms well; and
- does not exercise forbearance but puts banks into resolution as soon as they have reached the point of non-viability/fail to meet threshold conditions.

Such monitoring and minding activities reduce the probability that the bank will fail. They also reduce loss given resolution. Therefore, investors and ultimately banks are likely to value supervisory regimes that are inquisitive monitors and pro-active minders, for these traits will lead to lower expected loss to investors. That in turn could lead to lower funding costs for banks. As a result, banks may find it advantageous to race, not to the bottom, but to the top, that is, to seek out superior supervision.[2]

Two aspects of supervision deserve emphasis. First, regulation will require banks to manage themselves on a legal vehicle basis as well as on a consolidated (group-wide) and line-of-business basis. So will investors, for in a world where bail-in rather than bail-out is the rule, the investor's risk depends on the health of the legal vehicle within the banking group on which the investor has a claim as well as the investor's position in the "waterfall" that would allocate loss, if that legal entity and/or other members of the banking group were to enter resolution.

Second, supervisors are demanding data that are both very granular and very frequent as input to enable supervisors to monitor banks' condition (e.g., via stress tests) and review banks' conduct (e.g., testing for compliance with rules against market abuse and money laundering). At the same time advances in technology make it possible to manage extremely large data sets at very low cost. Advances in analytics make it possible to increase efficiency and improve risk management. Spending to meet supervisory demands should ideally form the basis for shifting banks' operations away from function-specific legacy systems housed in separate silos to a more integrated, more flexible and more efficient system that supports both business and supervisory requirements (see "Technology" later).

Meeting the strategic challenge

Although supervision may add value, and regulation and supervision may represent good business practice, the fact remains that the increase in capital and liquidity requirements threatens – all else equal – to reduce banks' return on equity (RoE) (see Figure 5.2).

All other things equal, the increase in capital requirements will force the banks to reduce leverage (assets/equity or A/E). If the return on assets (RoA) does not change, this will reduce RoE (see arrow 1 in Figure 5.2). The reform to resolution regimes will raise funding costs. The end of "too big to fail" and the removal of the associated implicit guarantee mean that banks will have to fund at the lower

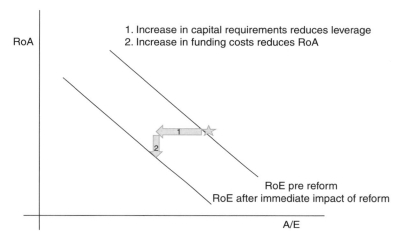

Figure 5.2 Regulatory reform requires strategic response

stand-alone rating. That will be more expensive, at least for weak banks headquartered in jurisdictions with fiscally robust governments (see Chapter 1). Again, all else equal, this implies a reduction in RoA and therefore a reduction in RoE (see arrow 2 in Figure 5.2).

The strategic challenge facing each bank is to make sure this is not the end of the story. Yes, the bank will have to comply with the new regulations. Yes, the bank will have to make itself resolvable. But the bank also needs to serve its customers. And the bank will have to do so in the context of a rapidly evolving market for financial services with the threat of increased competition from new entrants and growing market power from issuers and investors, particularly in wholesale markets. Finally, the bank has to find a way to serve its shareholders as well: over time the bank needs to earn a return on equity that exceeds its cost of equity capital.

To meet all these objectives simultaneously, the bank needs to take a fresh look at its business – just as investors will be doing. This entails:

- Setting sustainable targets for risk and return
- Rethinking the business model
- Choosing where to compete
- Developing what it takes to win in the market

Setting sustainable targets for risk and return

The first step in meeting this strategic challenge is to recalibrate the targets for risk and return. Banks must set sustainable targets, that is, ones that are consistent with the new regulatory environment *and with each other* whilst at the same time meeting the requirements of shareholders and customers.

Regulation and supervision effectively rule out banks' attempting to pursue a high-risk strategy. The authorities are effectively aiming to require banks to maintain an investment-grade stand-alone rating even at the trough of the business cycle at least at the operating bank subsidiary. Shareholders effectively rule out banks' pursuing a minimal return strategy – over time, banks must earn the cost of equity capital.

That leaves banks with a range of possible risk and return targets to choose from (see Figure 5.3). But banks need to

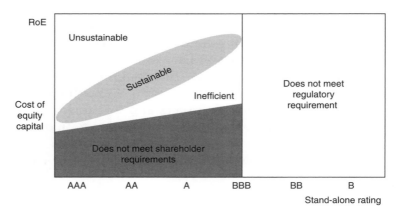

Figure 5.3   Banks need to set sustainable target for risk and return

choose a combination – the return target should be consistent with the risk target. They cannot set the return target independently from the risk target.

Prior to the crisis, many banks did just that. The return target was not sustainable, for it was not consistent with the risk target. Banks targeted RoE at 20 per cent or more while stating that they would simultaneously maintain a credit rating of AA or better. Some banks achieved this at the peak of the cycle, but when the crash came, profits plummeted and ratings collapsed. In many cases, the bank in question had to seek public assistance. The combination of high RoE and low risk proved unsustainable.

Although the lower risk imposed by the regulatory environment may imply a lower target RoE, it need not imply lower returns to shareholders.[3] That depends primarily on whether the return on equity exceeds the cost of equity, not on the absolute rate of return on equity. Bigger RoE is not necessarily better RoE (see Figure 5.4). If the bank takes high risk, it will have a high cost of equity capital. With lower risk, the bank will have a lower cost of equity capital. Getting over the

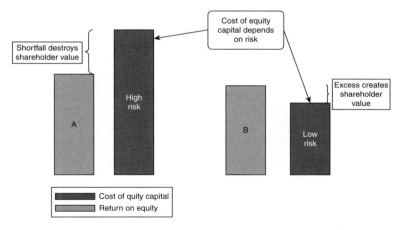

Figure 5.4   Creating shareholder value

bar (the cost of equity capital) is what creates shareholder value, not how high one jumps. The RoE under the high-risk strategy (A in Figure 5.4) may be higher than the RoE (B) under the low-risk strategy. But the former will destroy shareholder value (A is less than the cost of equity capital), whilst the latter will create shareholder value (B is greater than the cost of equity capital). In other words, what matters is the distance by which the bank clears the bar, not only how high it jumps. Consequently, lowering the bar (the cost of equity capital) by lowering risk can be an effective means to improve shareholder value, especially if coupled with measures to increase efficiency (and so raise return on equity).[4]

Rethinking the business model

The next and perhaps most important step in meeting the strategic challenge is to rethink the business model. As in other businesses, technology is leading to a disaggregation of banking into its fundamental components: intermediation and services. Within these components, competition is arising at each point along the value chain, and banks will need to decide at what points of the value chain and in which markets they wish to compete and develop what it takes to win in each of those markets.

The typical picture of a bank – the one reflected in Figure 5.2 and the one presented by banks themselves and investment analysts – is essentially an asset view. It focuses on the bank as investor in a portfolio of assets (principally loans and securities) funded by various liabilities (deposits, covered bonds, etc.). Banks earn a spread between the rate of return on their assets and the rate they pay on their liabilities, and leverage multiplies this spread to produce an RoE that may be satisfactory to shareholders.

Alternatively, one can take an activity view of the bank. This is far more dynamic, and focuses more on the value that banks provide to customers and the income such activities generate. Assets are secondary to the story – they are akin to the inventory that retailers hold in order to facilitate sales, and they should be subject to the same type of management (see "Increasing efficiency").

Banks engage in two types of activity: intermediation and services (see Figure 5.5 and Box 5.1). As intermediaries, banks bring together issuers and investors, acting either as agent (adviser/broker) or as principal (market-maker or risk-transformer). As service providers, banks execute a number of functions, either in support of capital market activities (e.g., clearing and settlement, custody) or in connection with payments (e.g., cash management). Within many of these functions, economies of scale prevail or network effects exist, thanks principally to technology. But technology also permits the entry of new players as well an increase in the market power of issuers and investors. This puts pricing pressure on the market for the bank's services.

As the value chain disaggregates, so may the bank's activities separate into distinct businesses, each with its own market. Banks face a choice regarding whether to make or buy each component of the value chain and if they decide to make, do they also try to sell the service or product to third parties? For many of these separate businesses, there are significant economies of scale as well as learning by doing or experience effects. As a result, such services tend to cluster around a relatively small number of providers, who compete with each other on the basis of technology, price and service enhancement. For example, in the case of loans, a bank can turn to third parties to buy either the loan itself, or to buy services that are essentially components of the loan or links in the value chain. It can turn to brokers for assistance in origination; and to loan servicers for the collection of interest and amortisation payments (see Figure 5.5).

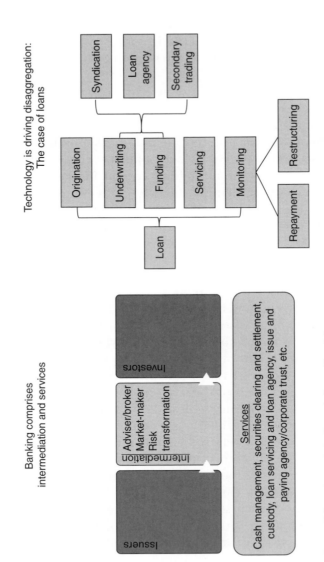

Figure 5.5 An activity-based view of banking

Box 5.1   Banks as intermediaries

Banks act as intermediaries in three different capacities, each of which is subject to increasing competition:

1. *As adviser or broker.* The bank facilitates the completion of a transaction between buyer and seller by acting as the adviser to or agent for either the buyer or the seller. The bank does not commit its own capital to the transaction, but does need to make investments in talent and technology to be able to provide advice and/or execution in the time frame required by the client. Examples of such activity include:
   a. merger and acquisition advice: here, talent-based specialist advisers are providing increased competition. In addition, frequent buyers of such advice (e.g., private equity houses, large firms) are building their own capabilities. This both limits the scope for banks to provide advice and strengthens the buyer's negotiating power.
   b. Stock brokerage: here, technology-based firms are providing increased competition, principally by offering an execution-only service. This has undermined the full-service brokerage model that bundled advice and research with execution. In addition, frequent buyers of brokerage services, such as hedge funds and large asset managers, have considerable negotiating power as well as in some cases an ability to cross trades in house (as so avoid using the bank's brokerage services at all).

2. *As market-maker.* The bank acts as principal. It buys an instrument (e.g., a corporate bond) from the seller (issuer). The bank sells that same instrument to a buyer (investor). If the seller is issuing the instrument for the first time, the bank may underwrite (provide a firm commitment to buy) the instrument.

   The value of market-making to customers is liquidity: immediacy and certainty of execution at a price close to immediately preceding transactions. To generate this value, the market maker must stand ready to acquire instruments in the amount that sellers (issuers) wish to sell, even if the market-maker does not immediately have a buyer ready, willing and able to buy. To do so, the market-maker must have the requisite capacity, both in terms of capital and exposure limits, to take very large positions very quickly into the bank's inventory. The market-maker must also stand ready to sell instruments in the amount that buyers (investors) wish to buy. To do so, the market-maker must maintain an inventory of the instrument in question. This enables the market maker to fulfil the customer's buy order immediately.

However, the whole point of market-making is to assure that the positions don't stay in inventory – rather that they turn over, much the way groceries do on supermarket shelves. Indeed, if positions get stuck in a market-maker's inventory, this will compromise its ability to take on new transactions or make new underwriting commitments. The income earned by the market-maker is principally the difference between the price at which the bank sells the instrument and the price at which the bank bought the instrument, not the "carry" or net interest differential between the yield on the assets in inventory and the cost of financing such assets.[5]

3. *As risk-transformer.* Here the bank transforms the instrument that the issuer (seller) wants to sell into an instrument that the investor (buyer) wants to buy. There are two separate transactions, one with the issuer (seller) and one with the investor (buyer) and the bank acts as principal in each. The bank is counterparty to the issuer and the bank is counterparty to the investor.

Risk transformation is most appropriate where there is little or no actively traded market in the instrument(s) concerned. The most common example of risk transformation is long-term loans financed by short-term deposits. The bank takes the credit risk on the borrower; the depositor (or the deposit guarantee scheme) takes the credit risk on the bank. In addition, as a result of the difference in maturity the bank takes liquidity and interest rate risk. And if the loan is denominated in a currency different from the currency of the deposit, the bank will take foreign exchange risk.

However, this risk transformation is not an end in itself. What counts in the eyes of the borrower is the ability to get financing when it wishes or needs to do so. Once the loan is made, the borrower is generally less concerned with who actually holds the loan. Indeed, the borrower will generally prefer that the bank retain the capacity (under capital and liquidity requirements and legal lending limits) to make new loans to the borrower, especially under revolving credit or backstop liquidity agreements.

Choosing where to compete

In rethinking its business model, the bank needs to decide where it will compete: which customers will it serve, which products will it offer and which geographic markets will it cover?

The bank should base this decision on a thorough understanding of the risks that the business model will require the bank to assume. Indeed, much of the return that a bank earns stems from compensation for bearing risks that neither issuers nor investors wish to assume. The bank should thoroughly analyse all the risks that it will be taking,[6] and assure that it is in fact getting paid a market rate of return for such risks.[7] In addition, the bank must be able to allocate to the business the minimum amount of risk capacity that the business will require in order to compete effectively with others in the market.[8] Indeed, the bank should only consider staying in or entering a market, if it has sufficient appetite (and risk capacity to support that appetite) over a full credit or business cycle.

For existing firms, the choice of where to compete is effectively a "stay and/or go" decision:

- stay with or go from the firm's existing customers/products/ markets; and/or
- go to new customer/product/market segments.

In taking this decision, banks should take into account how markets are today and how they are likely to evolve, both with respect to the size and rate of growth of the market's revenue pool and with respect to the profit potential that the market affords. Note that the "go from" aspect of the analysis is particularly important: strategy is as much about deciding what the bank will not do, as it is about deciding what the bank will do.

The financial services revenue pool

Today, the financial services "revenue pool" is predominantly in developed economies and predominantly in banking rather than capital markets. Ten to fifteen years from now there is likely to be a very different picture.

First, there will be a shift to emerging markets. These economies are likely to continue to grow much more rapidly than developed economies, and as they do, financial deepening (an increase in financial services relative to GDP) will most probably occur. As a result, today's emerging markets are likely to account for a much larger portion of a much larger global financial services revenue pool (see Figure 5.6).

However, this growth is not likely to be either uniform across emerging markets or constant across time. Risks of reversal remain, particularly if political development does not support economic development.[9] Even in cases where it does, growth may hit speed bumps (e.g., as the economy shifts from investment to consumption). And at some point growth will decelerate. As an emerging economy catches up with the developed world, growth has to come from extending the frontier of technology. This may well be a slower process than adopting modern technology and techniques.

Second, there will be a shift to capital markets. As economies grow and financial deepening occurs, investors seek greater returns than bank deposits typically provide, particularly if investors increasingly use institutions such as mutual funds and pension funds to make investment decisions on their behalf. Technology provides a further impetus toward capital markets, as does the improvement in analytics. This makes it easier for issuers to disseminate and investors to access the information needed in order to assess the risk of the issuer as counterparty, borrower or as an equity investment. And improvements in technology foster the development of infrastructures (securities settlement systems central counterparties, exchanges, etc.) and services (e.g., custody, funds administration, issuing and paying agency) necessary to support capital markets.

Although much of the growth in capital markets will occur in emerging markets, there is still considerable scope for growth in developed markets, especially Europe, where

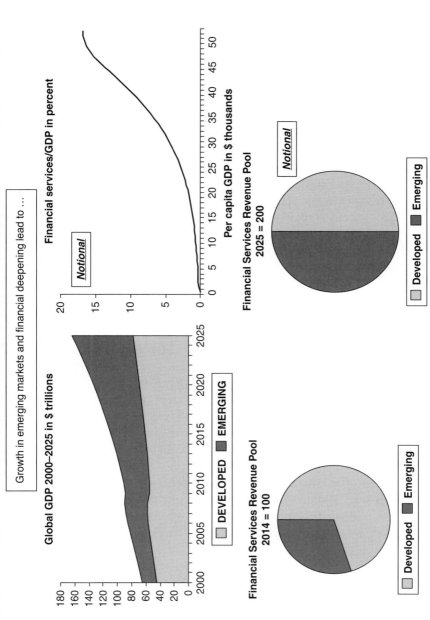

Figure 5.6 Emerging economies drive growth in financial services

bank lending remains the principal source of finance for institutions and individuals.

Third, clients are likely to accumulate clout, particularly in wholesale markets. Institutional investors such as asset managers and sovereign wealth funds already account for a growing share of total investment and trading. Such entities have the size and scope to take in-house many of the functions that banks have traditionally performed. Clients are not only conducting their own research and analysis, but they are also structuring portfolios via leverage and derivatives to implement specific investment strategies. This pushes banks towards an execution-only role, where margins are lower. On the "issuer" side "repeat" customers, such as private equity investors, tend to have more bargaining power and more bargaining expertise. This tends to put pressure on underwriting fees as well as on fees for M&A advice.

Consumers will have considerable clout as well, particularly in developed economies, principally as a result of actions by the authorities responsible for conduct regulation and supervision. These authorities are not only tightening implementation of long-standing regulations (e.g., rules to assure suitability, prevent churning, control conflicts of interest and protect client money), but they are also beginning to test whether or not consumers get the "right" outcomes (see "Conduct regulation and supervision" in Chapter 3). In effect, the supervisor is increasingly acting to assure that the consumer gets a fair deal.

In sum, the financial services revenue pool is likely to undergo significant changes over the next ten years. Although the overriding trends – the shift to emerging markets and the shift to capital markets – can be forecast with a reasonable degree of confidence, the exact details will depend on a number of factors, not least the pace and duration of the recovery in industrialised countries that may now be getting under way, and the choices that G-SIBs themselves make in the coming years with respect to specific products and markets.

Assessing profit potential

In choosing where to compete the bank must consider not only potential growth in the revenue pool but potential profit that the market could generate overall and the portion that might be available to the bank. That will depend on the structure of the market and the position of the bank.

The structure of the markets in which banks compete is changing rapidly. As outlined earlier, technology is driving the disaggregation of financial functions into separate markets. Within many of these markets, technology is giving rise to economies of scale and to network effects. Firms that have large market shares and their costs under control (see "Increasing efficiency" later) will enjoy significant profit margins. These in turn can provide the funding for continued investment necessary to enhance services and expand capacity to handle increased volumes of transactions.

For firms in the market that do not already have significant market shares, the strategic question is whether to remain in the market, exit the market entirely or seek another position on the value chain in line with the firm's comparative advantage. With a small market share, it may be difficult for a firm to generate profits in that market, especially if there are high fixed costs to assemble the combination of talent and technology necessary to be credible in the eyes of the client. If there is little or no prospect of achieving critical mass in terms of market share, the firm should consider exiting the business, ideally via a sale to a third party that would permit it to realise the value of its current book of business and current customer relationships.

Global custody provides an excellent example of this process at work. Over time there has been a considerable consolidation within the industry, driven largely by massive capital investments in technology and acquisitions of smaller players (who could not afford to make such investments) by the larger.

For firms that are not already in a market, the question is whether to enter or not. It makes sense to do so, if the firm can see a way to capitalise on its current capabilities and if the firm can gain permission to enter the market. Not all of these potential entrants will be banks. Indeed, banks, too, are likely to face their "Spotify moment,"[10] or disruptive innovation that changes the basis on which firms must compete. In fact, this may already be happening in payments and loans, the very core of traditional banking (see Box 5.2).[11]

Box 5.2   What to do about loans

In the eyes of many, lending and banking are synonymous. Indeed, in some jurisdictions, banks have been defined as institutions that make loans and take deposits. Yet loans are increasingly taking on many of the properties of securities. Increasingly, many investors participate in a single loan. Increasingly, these investors are not banks, and increasingly these investors trade the loan participations in secondary markets.

Nor are banks necessary to originate loans. The advent of peer-to-peer lending platforms allows issuers (borrowers) to post requests for credit directly to prospective investors and to furnish such investors with the information that allows the investor to analyse the credit and make an investment decision.

As yet, such lending platforms are in their infancy. But they plainly have the potential to disintermediate banks. This has significant implications, not least for the banks behind the ring-fence (see Chapter 2) separating commercial and investment banking.

Both banks and regulators have to recognise that loan platforms are likely to develop into full marketplaces. As they do, questions will arise as to whether issuers (borrowers) are obliged to follow the same disclosure rules as the issuers of securities, and whether investors in loans are obliged to follow the same rules regarding market abuse. Questions will also arise as to the obligations of the operators of such platforms, whether they are agents or underwriters, and what liability they have concerning the correctness of the credit rating that platforms assign to loans.

The challenge facing banks is how to interface with such platforms. Does the bank set up its own platform? Does (can) the bank invest in loans requested by issuers (borrowers) over a third-party platform? Does the bank set up a reverse offer platform, publishing its underwriting standards and inviting borrowers who meet them to submit bids? Does (can) the bank package its own loans and sell participations in such loans to investors (effectively a pass-through securitisation)?[12]

This range of questions should be enough to indicate that the traditional separation between loans and securities will blur, and that it may be possible for banks to originate loans and sell them directly to investors without having to hold the loans on their balance sheet. If so, earnings for banks would come primarily from origination fees to issuers, from distribution fees to investors and transaction fees. The inventory of loans that banks would keep on their balance sheet could be much smaller (as would be the associated capital and liquidity requirements).

In addition to developing a strategy in response to loan platforms, banks will also need to rethink securitisation. Properly done, securitisation allows banks to concentrate on their core strength of origination and underwriting, whilst investors hold the asset (removing the need for the bank to hold the asset on its balance sheet and to finance the asset). In essence, this was the motivation for the so-called originate to distribute strategy.

In practice, however, many banks failed to distribute. They retained portions of securitisation issues, not to have "skin in the game" but to gain what they believed were superior returns for particular tranches in the securitisation structures. In some cases, banks went beyond retaining some portion of the loans that they themselves had originated. They started to buy loans from others, so that "originate to distribute" became "acquire to arbitrage" – a strategy that led to immense losses at several G-SIBs in 2007 and 2008.[13]

This time around, banks will have to distribute more fully. That remained largely the case even during the crisis with respect to securitisations based on credit card receivables. Here, issuers devoted considerable time and effort in developing an investor base that understood the characteristics of the underlying credits, could analyse the cash flows and assess the underwriting performance of the sponsor. Banks need to apply these same disciplines to securities backed by other classes of assets, including mortgages on residential and commercial real estate as well as to commercial loans, including loans to small- to medium-sized enterprises (SMEs).

Banks will also need to simplify structuring. Rather than embed derivatives in the securitisation itself, banks will need to consider returning to something akin to straight pass-through securities. If the investor wants protection against interest rate, credit and/or liquidity risk s/he can contract for that separately. Fewer tranches are also likely to work better: a simple senior, subordinated, stub scheme is much easier to analyse and administer.

Finally, banks will have to improve disclosure. They will need to inform investors on the performance of the loans or assets in the pool underlying the securitisation issue, not only at origination but during the entire life of the security. An important feature of such disclosure will be the assurance that the borrowers actually conform to the underwriting standards set by the bank and/or to the standards mandated by any guarantor of the underlying assets in the pool. This will require banks to exercise stricter controls over origination (especially where banks rely on third parties such as mortgage brokers) and to furnish investors with the same type of detailed information on borrowers and property that supervisors are demanding from banks in connection with stress tests.

In sum, securitisation deserves resurrection as a tool on the bank's workbench. Provided the "distribute" leg works well, and the bank complies with strict controls on conduct and credit in the "originate" leg, "originate to distribute" is a fine strategy. With proper execution it can be a fine strategy again.

Developing what it takes to win in the market

In addition to choosing where to compete, banks have to develop what it takes to win, both in individual markets and overall as a firm. Four qualities stand out:

- The bank needs to be under control.
- The bank needs to be resilient.
- The bank needs to be efficient.
- The bank needs to be flexible.

Talent and technology hold the key to the bank's achieving these outcomes.

Being under control
The best brakes and the best steering are frequently found in sports cars. Indeed, without excellent controls it is inadvisable

to drive at high speeds. The same principle holds true for banks. Without very good controls the bank will find it difficult to compete. At one point or another, poor controls will result in losses of capital, liquidity and/or reputation. When such losses do crystallise, they will divert management's attention from building the business to dealing with the problem or even to making sure the bank survives. By then, it may be too late to save the bank.

Creating better controls will reduce the probability that the bank suffers extreme losses, increase the stability of earnings and, together with the reduction in leverage, improve the bank's stand-alone rating. Controls comprise the ability to set the bank's direction as well as the ability to keep the bank on course.

Setting the bank's direction: establishing risk appetite

Good controls start with controlling the bank's risk appetite. This sets the direction that the bank should take. Boards need to assure that the bank's risk appetite is in line with the bank's risk capacity while recognising that the bank has to be able to take a minimum level of risk if it is to compete successfully in various lines of business.[14] The critical task is to assure that risk appetite remains within risk capacity. The practical tasks are to determine how much of a buffer the firm should have between capacity and appetite and the steps the firm could take if capacity contracts.

Determining the bank's risk capacity is the first step, for this sets a limit on how much risk the bank could take. Roughly defined, "risk capacity" is the amount of money (in absolute terms) that the bank could afford to lose without reaching the point of non-viability, or some higher threshold (such as the inability to pay dividends) as may be defined by shareholders. Note that this amount is likely to be quite sensitive to the interaction between capital and liquidity. If small losses in capital lead to rapid significant losses in liquidity (case 1 in Figure 5.7), risk capacity will be much smaller than

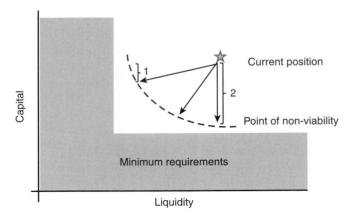

Figure 5.7 Calculating risk capacity

if the bank is able to retain liquidity even as it loses capital (case 2 in Figure 5.7).

Risk appetite indicates how much of that capacity the bank wishes to utilise. In the long run, the bank's risk appetite cannot exceed its risk capacity. If risk capacity does contract (as it would, if the bank experienced a loss), the bank will very likely face a difficult choice. It either needs to restore capacity or reduce its risk appetite. The former may require the issuance of new capital and possibly lead to dilution. The latter (reducing risk appetite) can pose strategic challenges for the bank. To remain competitive in various lines of business, a bank must be prepared to take certain amounts of risk. For example, a bank will not remain effective as a market maker for very long if it stops bidding for deals in the amounts that clients expect to be able to buy or sell. Nor will a bank remain able to compete in the credit card market if it substantially cuts back customers' limits relative to financially sound peers.

Consequently, in setting risk appetite, a bank should leave a considerable cushion between capacity and appetite (see Figure 5.8). The bank should also plan on how to

Risk Capacity	The maximum level of risk the firm can assume before it reaches the point of non-viability, breaches regulatory constraints (e.g. capital, liquidity) or other stakeholders' constraints (e.g. dividend pay-out).
Risk Appetite	The aggregate level and types of risk a firm is willing to assume in its exposures in order to achieve it business objectives.

Buffer	One issue is how big the buffer between appetite and capacity should be. The buffer should consider possibility of very extreme outcomes and modelling error.
Risk Appetite Framework	The framework of policies and processes that establish and monitor adherence to the firm's risk appetite.
Risk Appetite Statement	An outline of the aggregate levels and types of risk a firm is willing to accept to achieve its business objectives.

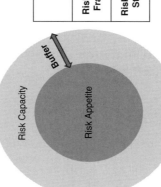

Figure 5.8 Setting a buffer between risk capacity and appetite

build capacity, both gradually through earnings retention and/or balance sheet management in order to build a basis for growth, as well as rapidly, if the bank needs to restore capacity after suffering a loss (see "Remaining resilient" later). If the bank's recovery plan affords it few such options, it should build in a higher buffer between risk capacity and risk appetite.

Controlling risk appetite cannot stop with the top-down exercise outlined earlier. To be effective a risk appetite framework has to capture all risks and it has to cascade the bank's risk appetite in a consistent manner from the group level down to individual businesses. This requires the bank to establish a common risk language across different business. That should be the language of loss in absolute terms – the euros, dollars or pounds that the bank could lose if the risks were to crystallise.

The bank then needs to use this common language to analyse each of the risks that it assumes. This is fairly straightforward for quantifiable risks such as credit, market and interest rate risk, but it is more difficult – but no less important – with respect to conduct risks. Indeed, given the recent escalation in fines and requirements for restitution as well as the possible suspension or revocation of some or all of the bank's licenses, banks need to assign high priority to analysing the losses that could result from conduct risk (see Box 5.3).

Box 5.3   Scoring conduct risk

Another challenge will be to demonstrate how the bank can fulfil qualitative statements relating to areas such as conduct risk and operating risk. Typically such statements indicate that the bank will not suffer losses from such risks. How can the bank provide assurance to the board, to supervisors and ultimately to investors that it will not in fact suffer losses from conduct and/or operating risk? How good are the controls with respect to unauthorised trading or mis-selling?

Should the line managers making such qualitative statements be asked to post a percentage of revenues as a bond that the business unit will in fact fulfil its commitment to avoid losses from such risks? Should the firm take a similar or greater reserve against revenues and pass this into profit only after it is clear that the bank will not be required to disgorge past revenues or profits as a result of customer complaints and/or enforcement actions?

One approach is to develop a score for conduct risk, similar to the scoring for credit risk that was developed decades ago. This would include ranking the business or product against factors that frequently give rise to conduct issues, including without limitation the sophistication of the customer, the complexity of the product, the level of training of the staff, and so on. The score would be a composite of the individual characteristics. (For example, using untrained staff to sell complex products to unsophisticated clients would score highly and is likely to result in conduct issues.)

A second and complementary approach is to monitor adherence to the original product approval criteria, especially where the product is growing rapidly and/or is generating extraordinary profits. Frequently, such success results from marketing the product to a much broader group than the one for whom the product was originally intended. Or the success may result from improper or even criminal behaviour (insider trading would be an example). If things are too good to be true, there is usually something wrong.

Finally, the bank needs to allocate its aggregate risk appetite among the line businesses. In doing so, the bank should resist the temptation to assume significant diversification among businesses and to allocate risk appetites (and therefore potential losses) to businesses in excess of the risk appetite for the group as a whole. Experience has shown that in a stress environment, risks tend to become more highly correlated. When it counts, there is little or no diversification benefit to be had. Consequently, the sum of the risk appetites granted to individual businesses should be no higher than the risk appetite for the bank as a whole.

Assuring the bank remains on course: Three lines of defence

As any driver, pilot or sailor knows, setting direction is no guarantee that one will arrive safely at the desired destination. One has to take measures to assure that one stays on course, and one has to catch and correct any errors as quickly as possible, for small deviations from the correct course can cast the vessel or vehicle widely adrift of where it needs to be.

The same is true of banking. Keeping on course is what gets the bank to the right destination – a sustainable rate of return. To do so banks have developed the "three lines of defense" model, namely (1) business management, (2) risk management and compliance, and (3) internal audit. In concept, this is an excellent model. The trick is putting it into practice, so that the bank has an effective risk culture.

The key line of defence is the first line. Business management has to accept that it is responsible for risk as well as return, just as drivers take command of the brakes and steering wheel as well as the gas pedal. Does control start with business management, so that executives balance return and risk? Does business management base compensation and career progression decisions on whether executives control risk and assure compliance as well as whether executives increase revenues and build market share? That is essentially the litmus test for an effective risk culture. If control does not start with business management, it is extremely unlikely that the other two lines of defence can offset this.

The second line of defence is "risk management and compliance." This second line has primary responsibility for designing the risk appetite framework and implementing the risk appetite statement, including the allocation of risk appetite to individual business units and the development of an appropriate limit structure. It further controls that business management is adhering to those limits, ideally in advance of commitments being given to clients. Finally, risk management needs to keep its techniques and technology up to date as well as to scan the horizon for risks that could – if they were to crystallise – have a material adverse impact on the bank.

The role of compliance is threefold. It needs to assure that the bank is adhering to all the relevant rules and regulations in each of the jurisdictions in which the bank operates. If breaches do occur, compliance needs to assure that the bank is taking the appropriate remedial action, that the bank conducts a root cause analysis and that the bank takes steps to correct the conditions that contributed to the breach. Additionally, compliance needs to work with business management and risk management to put in place controls that will either prevent breaches entirely or deliver a warning signal to the bank that a breach might occur (see Box 5.3). This will allow the bank to take preventive measures in a timely manner so that it does not stray off course. Finally, compliance, like risk management, needs to think ahead. If possible, it needs to imagine how society in the future might view practices of the present – which ones will the future condemn if they come into the full light of day?

The third line of defence is internal audit (IA). Briefly put, its role is to assure that the first two lines of defence are operating as they should.[15] To this end, its audit plan should focus on high-risk areas but be comprehensive enough to cover the entire bank within a reasonable period of time. Of particular importance is the interaction between internal audit and line management. The starting point for internal audit's review should be an assessment of management's awareness of the risks in the business s/he is running, the state of the control environment and the probable effectiveness of any mitigation measures already employed. The ending point for internal audit's review is how the bank's line management regards audit's report. Does the business view the report as useful feedback, develop and implement in a timely manner the appropriate corrective action program? Does the bank's senior management regard failing an audit as the equivalent of a parking violation, or as a reason to limit compensation or even career progression?

Remaining resilient

Even if the bank is under control, it may nonetheless encounter turbulence, much the way an airplane that has passed pre-flight inspection can encounter problems during a flight. External conditions may be more adverse than expected, controls may have failed and/or the "pilot" (i.e., the bank's senior management) may have committed an error.

Remaining resilient in the face of such turbulence is vital if the bank is to survive. That is the purpose of recovery planning – an exercise which G-SIBs as well as many other banks are required to conduct (see Chapter 3). From a strategic point of view, such recovery planning makes perfect sense. Indeed, if a bank does not have an array of credible, feasible recovery options, it should consider maintaining a larger buffer between risk capacity and risk appetite. Over the longer term, it should consider means to increase its resiliency.

Of particular importance is an effective contingency funding plan. This can give the bank the room it needs to take more fundamental corrective measures, such as raising capital or making a divestiture. Without such a plan, the bank could quickly run out of liquidity, reach the point of non-viability and be forced into resolution. As emphasised earlier (see Chapter 3), a critical component of such a plan is what might be termed a collateral budget – sources and uses of collateral at the bank's disposal, with particular emphasis on unencumbered assets eligible for discount at central bank(s) under normal lending facilities.

Increasing efficiency

Efficiency is the key to profitability and to assuring that the bank can earn a return on equity that exceeds its cost of equity capital. Two aspects of efficiency deserve emphasis: efficiency in the use of assets, and efficiency with respect to cost.

Asset efficiency

Under the activity approach outlined earlier assets serve the same purpose as inventory does in a retail store – they are there to facilitate sales, not as a business in their own right. Increasing the turnover ratio (revenues/assets) should therefore be a priority. To do so, the bank can seek either to reduce assets or to increase the revenues to which each euro of assets contributes (over and above the return that the asset itself generates). If the bank can reduce assets, it will need less funding and possibly less CET1 capital. If so, that will improve RoA and RoE.

Why should this be possible? Briefly put, there are two reasons. First, the bank may cull its involvement in various businesses as a result of its strategic review (see "Choosing where to compete"). Such a review should lead the bank to exit loss-making or marginal businesses and to focus on businesses in which they have competitive advantage. This rebalancing should result in higher return on assets and may free up capital.

Second, it should be possible to improve the efficiency of the assets that banks hold in connection with the businesses in which they do decide to compete. The key question the bank should be asking is "Does holding the asset do anything to promote further business with clients"? The answer is clearly yes for some businesses (holding an appropriate inventory of securities to facilitate market-making is an example) but for many businesses, the rationale for holding assets can be questioned. Indeed, for some businesses, such as corporate finance, it may be more important for the bank to retain the capacity to respond positively to new credit requests from a client than for the bank to finance the client's already outstanding debt. The bank will not be able to respond positively (i) if existing claims on a particular client exhaust the bank's legal lending limit or its internal exposure guidelines, or (ii) if existing claims on clients in aggregate strain the bank's ability to meet capital and/or liquidity requirements. To retain the ability to originate (respond to demands for new credit), the bank may need to place outstanding credit with investors. This suggests that banks may wish to revisit the "originate to distribute" strategy.[16]

For assets that do not promote further business with clients, the bank should ask, "Is this bank the best holder of the asset"? For some assets, this may well be the case. For example, it may well make sense for the bank to hold loans (especially in the form of overdrafts) to firms or individuals where the bank also has the client's primary current or cash management account. Such deposit account relationships potentially provide the bank with a de facto first claim on any cash the client might receive (and this will be used to reduce any overdraft the client might have). Such accounts may also provide the bank with superior real-time insight into how the client's credit standing is developing.

But many of the assets which banks carry in their inventory (on their balance sheet) are simply investments, part of what might be called an "acquire to arbitrage" strategy.[17] Such assets do little or nothing to promote further business with clients or add to revenue over and above what the asset yields.[18] Although such "idle" inventory may have a negative cost to carry (in other words, the bank earns a spread between the rate of return on the asset portfolio and the all-in cost of funding), the bank may not be the best owner of such assets. Other investors may be better placed to hold the assets, especially if they are exempt from corporate taxation.

A rigorous transfer pricing regime can contribute significantly to asset efficiency. In such a regime the bank's central treasury unit would act effectively as an internal bank – paying a market rate of interest to businesses with excess funds and charging a market rate of interest to businesses (i.e., one that is related to the risk of the business rather than the risk of the bank as a whole) that require funds, whilst keeping in treasury the pool of liquid assets required for the group to meet its liquidity requirements. In such a transfer pricing system, it is particularly important that businesses be charged a fee for the liquidity demands that they might place on the central treasury unit as a result of the liquidity commitments that the business gives to clients. Such a transfer pricing system should also extend to collateral. This will support the development of an overall collateral budget for the bank and assure that the bank is putting collateral to its most efficient use. Finally, the transfer pricing regime should also extend to equity. The central treasury should consider charging each business a risk-adjusted cost for the equity capital allocated to the business. This will facilitate evaluation of business performance as well as help establish more rigorous compensation criteria (see "Creating key capabilities: talent" later).

Cost efficiency

In addition to assuring that it uses assets efficiently, the bank needs to assure that it manages its costs efficiently. Perhaps the best way to do so is to frame the question as a decision to invest in the system necessary to support the business:

- What is the return (in terms of margin or profit) on incurring the cost under consideration?
- Are there ways of configuring cost differently to yield a greater risk-adjusted return?

This investment approach has several advantages. First, it recognises that businesses are a system, a collection of people, processes and technology that should function as an integrated whole. Cutting costs in one area may not improve efficiency overall, if it creates bottlenecks elsewhere and/or leads to control failures. Second, the investment approach to the system as a whole builds on the discipline that should already be applicable to investments in technology (see "Creating key capabilities" later).

Fostering flexibility

Finally, banks will require flexibility if they are to win in the market.[19] They have to be able to respond to changes in market conditions, to the entry of new competitors and to advances in technology. In technical terms, banks need to create and preserve real options to enter and/or exit lines of business, introduce new products and employ new techniques. Such real options are vital, if the bank is to prosper and grow. Without such real options, a bank could wither and die.

The strategic challenge facing banks is to develop such options within the framework set by regulation and supervision, including the restrictions on bank structure (see Chapter 2). The bank's board and management need to assure that the bank can respond flexibly to changes in conditions. Is it locked into a market, condemned to take whatever price the market dictates, or does it have the capacity – thanks perhaps to diversification – to stop writing new business, if pricing becomes too low and/or risk becomes too great? In other words, boards should be asking whether the bank can continue to control its risk appetite if others in the industry lose their risk discipline. Does the bank's business model give it the option to take a temporary pause until market pricing again reflects the risk to the bank? If not, the review should ask whether this is a business that the bank can afford to be in.

From an opportunity perspective, does the bank have the financial and managerial capacity to take advantage of a major opportunity? If not, how can the bank build such a capacity?

Creating key capabilities

Talent and technology are the key capabilities that banks need to build in order to win in the markets in which they choose to compete. How banks build these capacities matters greatly, especially with respect to cost efficiency.

A critical consideration is whether the bank's talent and technology combine to create a learning organisation. Do the bank's processes reflect the accumulated experience of the bank regarding what works and what doesn't, so that routine matters can be handled routinely and time allocated to more complex matters that require judgement? Are the bank's processes subject to periodic review to assure that they remain effective and to permit the incorporation of new insights? Knowledge management (see "Technology" later) can help assure that banks can answer yes to both questions. Talent development can help assure that the bank asks the questions in the first place.

Talent

Banks unquestionably need qualified people. To use a regulatory phrase, bank staff need to be "fit and proper," and approved persons regimes in various jurisdictions are designed to assure that they are in fact so. But total compensation to employees can account for up to half of the bank's total operating expenses. So a bank needs to establish processes and incentives to assure that it is getting the most out of the talent it employs.

Clearly, incentives matter a great deal both to individuals and to the bank. They influence the behaviour and effort of employees, and bonus (the primary form of incentive) can account for the lion's share of total compensation expense, particularly for key employees. Getting incentives wrong can lead the bank to ruin, whilst getting them right can set the stage for success.

Regulation aims to prevent banks from getting incentives wrong, but banks will have to take steps of their own, if they are to get incentives right. As outlined in Chapter 2, regulation has done much to assure that compensation is consistent with effective risk management. When calculating a person's bonus, the bank cannot rely entirely on revenues or profit; it must now take the person's performance against risk and compliance objectives into account. When paying a bonus, the bank cannot pay it all-in cash. A significant portion must be paid in a performance-related instrument so that the person will suffer a loss if the bank's condition deteriorates markedly. Nor can the bank pay the entire bonus immediately. A significant portion of the bonus must be deferred. It should also be subject to claw-back, if it becomes apparent that there were flaws in the rationale for the bonus award.

However, banks will have to take steps of their own to get incentives right. In particular, banks will have to balance the interests of shareholders and employees. A rigorous transfer pricing system (see "Asset efficiency" earlier) would certainly help, for this would assure that the profit attributable to the business resulted after fully taking into account the cost of the equity capital necessary to support the business and after assuring that the business had assessed market rates for any funding received from any other business. Such a shift would help assure that bonus was paid on the basis of the economic profit the business had generated rather than simply reflect the amount of capital the business utilised or the internal negotiating power that the business may have vis-à-vis other areas of the bank.

Banks also need to think through the type and amount of talent they will require, as a product evolves or the business model changes. For example, as products "commoditize" (move along the spectrum from tailor-made to standardised), innovation (the specialty of the "master tailor") should give way to introducing "industrial" processes to assure appropriate controls and efficient handling of increased volumes.

Finally, banks need to consider the culture(s) that they are creating. In particular, banks need to consider what freedom should be allocated to different businesses within the group and what values should characterise the company as a whole. At one extreme is what might be called a "franchise" approach:

the group hires an executive to run a business and gives her carte blanche to hire her own team and set priorities. As long as the executive delivers her numbers (profit target), she will retain a free hand and "get to eat what she kills." Such an approach will tend to create silos. Unless these silos coincide with separate legal vehicles, each with its own controls, the franchise approach tends to transform transfer pricing into a power struggle and tends to undermine rather than promote an effective risk culture. Although some variance in culture may be appropriate from one business to another, executives and staff across the firm need to adhere to core values of integrity, commitment to clients and control of risk.

Technology

Technology is the other key capability that a bank must have. It encompasses not only hardware and software, but also processes and analytics. This broadly defined technology is central to running a bank, whether in retail or whole-sale banking. Technology enables the bank to perform its core functions of lending, payments, trading, risk management, compliance and so on. Without technology the bank could neither process the volume or range of transactions customers demand, nor generate and report the information that regulators and/or investors require. Nor could the bank manage its risk.

After compensation, technology broadly defined is the largest expense incurred by the bank. Until recently, major technology improvements have required massive capital investments. In theory these pay off in terms of greater revenue, better risk management and/or lower operating costs, but in practice these benefits have been hard to achieve and demonstrate, partly because much of the investment in technology (e.g., model development) is counted as current expense, and partly because many banks have deferred the hard task of integrating systems after mergers or acquisitions.

Two areas offer promise for improvement: data manage-
ment/analytics and the management of technology/opera-
tions within the bank. On data management, banks need to
consider how to make the most of the very extensive investments that they will be required to make to meet regulatory
requirements for data integrity, accuracy and timeliness
(see Chapter 2). Banks need to search for ways to make the
spending to meet mandatory regulatory requirements the
vehicle to improve their overall data management: to create
a single version of the truth (so that different data sets don't
have to be reconciled with one another), to automate hand-
offs from one system to another and so on. Banks also need
to find ways to use the vast amounts of data that they accumulate in the ordinary course of business to improve their
analytics.

Prospectively, the combination of technology and analytics
known as "Big Data" can help.[20] This allows firms to collect,
process, manage and analyse vast amounts of data extremely
quickly and very cheaply. This should enable banks to manage
risk and return more effectively, as well as enable banks to
keep pace with customer demands for faster and more accurate execution of transactions, especially payments and securities settlements.

Technology may also allow banks to make changes to their
systems more easily. With cloud computing and application
software, it may be possible to change the software once at
a central location rather than reprogram various systems
throughout the bank's network. Over time this should enable
banks to manage data more efficiently (e.g., reduce or eliminate the need to reconcile data from different systems),
conduct analyses more quickly and more thoroughly (e.g.,
score and control conduct risk) and take corrective action
more promptly.

In sum, better technology is likely to be the foundation
of better banking, particularly if the bank can effectively
combine technology and talent. To this end, the introduction

of a service subsidiary (OpCo) may help. Although the primary rationale for such an OpCo stems from work on resolution planning (see Chapter 4), an OpCo may be more important for banks in life than in death (resolution) for it can improve the technology investment process as well as simplify cost management in the line businesses and so potentially improve overall cost efficiency for the bank as a whole (see Box 5.4).

Box 5.4 How an OpCo can improve efficiency

In developing resolution plans banks and authorities developed the concept of an OpCo as a separately capitalised subsidiary that could continue to provide services to the rest of the group, even if one or more bank subsidiaries or the group as a whole entered resolution.

Even though other means are becoming available to assure continuity within resolution (see Chapter 4), banks may still find it sensible to create such an OpCo. The reason is two-fold: it may make management of technology more efficient, and it may make the bank's intermediation and services businesses more efficient.

The business model for OpCo differs from that for bank subsidiaries. The OpCo is a technology company. It should hold the group's intellectual property as well as the group's licenses from third parties. It should own the group's systems. The OpCo would sublicense these rights and systems to the bank subsidiaries and receive as revenues license and processing fees.

Like technology companies, OpCo is likely to have high fixed costs and low variable costs. The key issues relate to capital investment. Can the OpCo deliver solutions to the bank subsidiaries that will add new features, improve service quality and/or reduce cost? If so, will the license fees received from the bank subsidiary be sufficient to amortise the investment in the new technology?

Such a business model for OpCo would allow the bank subsidiary to shift more fully to a flow model, where it pays a volume related price for the services it accesses. The primary task of the bank executive would be to dimension the services the bank needs rather than analysing, creating and managing the technology the bank requires. The bank should also be able to negotiate a price with the OpCo, rather than being forced to accept an allocation that covers OpCo's costs. The investment risk (and reward) should remain with OpCo.

Transitioning to the new environment

Finally, banks must face the challenge of transitioning to the new environment. They have already made very significant additions to capital and liquidity. Many banks are already in compliance with the full Basel III requirements, especially with respect to risk-based capital. But banks still have a significant way to go in terms of meeting leverage requirements, building liquidity, strengthening risk management and improving controls. And many banks will continue to struggle with legacy issues – to wind down non-core businesses and to reach closure on enforcement and litigation proceedings stemming from the bank's conduct prior to and during the crisis.

To meet the transition challenge, it will be helpful to do three things: create a model of the business the bank is trying to become – does this work for shareholders as well as comply with regulation? Second, make the spending on talent and technology required to comply with regulation do double duty to build the bank's capacity to serve clients, control costs or improve risk management. Third, communicate the goal (the business model) and the progress towards meeting that goal clear to staff, supervisors, investors and the public at large.

Conclusion: Is Basel Best?

The crisis has changed banking. Even if the recovery takes hold, the days of "heads the bank wins, tails the public loses" are over. There will be no return to the pre-crisis regime. What will take its place? The Basel regime (less likely to fail, safe to fail) described in this book, or some other?

The Basel regime will enhance financial stability

The Basel regime is well on its way to implementation. Basel III has greatly strengthened regulation. The accord has prompted jurisdictions around the world to raise capital requirements, introduce liquidity requirements and set standards for governance and remuneration. This will reduce the likelihood that banks will fail.

So will efforts to sharpen supervision. In major jurisdictions around the world supervisors are becoming more forward-looking and more pro-active, both in monitoring banks and in intervening to keep banks away from the point of non-viability. Stress tests are playing a key role here – supervisors are insisting that banks have a capital buffer that would enable them to withstand a significant deterioration in economic conditions. As a practical matter, this has accelerated banks' compliance with the tougher capital standards imposed by Basel III. In sum, sharper supervision has complemented stronger regulation. Together, they reduce the risk that banks will fail.

There has also been extensive progress in making banks resolvable, or safe to fail, so that investors, not taxpayers, bear the cost of bank failures, and so that banks can continue to perform critical economic functions, even whilst they are in resolution. The FSB has identified the key attributes that resolution regimes should have, and jurisdictions around the world have taken steps to introduce such regimes. This establishes the framework in which effective resolution could take place.

Resolution plans translate the general framework into institution-specific blueprints that the authorities could follow, if the bank in question were to reach the point of non-viability and enter resolution. Broadly speaking, these plans indicate that banks can be made resolvable. Through bail-in investors could recapitalise the bank at the point of non-viability. That would assure the solvency of the bank-in-resolution and set the stage for it to obtain the liquidity it will require in order to continue in operation and to continue to perform critical economic functions.

To assure that this framework will actually function as designed, banks and the authorities will need to take three steps in advance. First, if investors are to recapitalise the bank at the point of non-viability, the bank must have a certain minimum amount of "reserve capital" outstanding. Accordingly, authorities are considering imposing requirements that banks issue "gone concern loss absorbing capital" (GLAC). Second, for the bank-in-resolution to obtain liquidity, it must have unencumbered assets that it could pledge to the liquidity provider as collateral. As part of liquidity regulation, banks will be required to track and report such assets. However, banks and authorities need to spell out in greater detail how the bank-in-resolution could in fact utilise such unencumbered assets to obtain liquidity. The first two steps would go a long way toward enabling the authorities to complete the third, namely, the establishment of "constructive certainty" about how they will work together to resolve a global banking group.[1]

These are doable tasks. But banks and the authorities need to stay the course if they are to secure the prize of making banks resolvable and thereby enhancing financial stability.

The Basel regime will challenge banks

Banks also need to determine how they will compete in the new environment. In a world where investors, not taxpayers, bear the cost of bank failures, banks can expect to come under increasing scrutiny from investors as well as supervisors. Accordingly, banks will have to set targets for return *and* risk that are sustainable. To achieve such targets banks will have to rethink their business models, increase their efficiency, strengthen their controls and augment their resiliency and flexibility. And they will have to improve the disclosure that they make not only to supervisors but to investors. Only then will they be able to remain competitive in a rapidly changing technological, economic and political environment.

This is admittedly a tall order. But it is arguably no taller than the challenges faced by many other industries (e.g., telecommunications, energy) facing rapid changes in technology, regulation and competition.[2]

What are the alternatives to Basel?

It is arguably a more conducive order than the one that could result if banks are deemed to be unresolvable. Banks should not expect, nor should society tolerate, a return to too big to fail. That is not only the path to fiscal folly and financial instability; it would in all likelihood also be the path – given the unpopularity of bankers – to the government's demise at the polls.

If banks are not deemed to be resolvable, they should expect a combination of much tougher regulation (so that they are even less likely to fail) and much more fragmentation (so that bank's operations within each national jurisdiction are "safe to fail").[3] Such measures would accelerate the shift of activity from banking markets to capital markets, but they would not necessarily make the financial system more stable.

Tougher regulation would very likely start with significantly stricter limits on leverage – something many would advocate even within the Basel regime. It would continue with further restrictions on the use of models and further reductions in the reliance on risk-weighted capital ratios.

If banks are deemed to be unresolvable, further fragmentation is practically a certainty. If global banks cannot become global in death, authorities will undoubtedly limit their ability to remain global in life. At a minimum, authorities will push global banks towards becoming national in life (as they would remain national in death). At a maximum, such national entities could face restrictions on inter-affiliate transactions, on officer and director interlocks, on opening foreign branches or engaging in international activities.[4]

But the effort of each jurisdiction to give priority to its own citizens cannot succeed. It is impossible for each country to have preference over the others within the group at the same time. The problem with the "my nation first" approach is simple. It ignores the rest of the world. But the rest of the world is increasingly relevant: trade continues to grow, as does cross-border investment. It is rash – as the example of Lehmans illustrates – to assume that the domestic economy will remain unaffected if resolution focuses solely on the domestic operations. If resolution of the group's foreign operations is disorderly, financial markets as a whole are likely to be affected adversely. This could well have repercussions on the domestic economy. Logically, therefore, nations should be interested in achieving a certain degree of coordination. Without such coordination, the effort of each jurisdiction to give priority to its own citizens and its own businesses will undermine rather than promote financial stability.

There could also be further constraints on banks' engaging in "non-traditional" activities, just at the time when traditional activities may begin to take "non-traditional" form (see Box 5.1 in Chapter 5). In other words, regulation could well take a course that would prevent banks from adapting to changes in technology or markets. Although this might be done in the name of financial stability, anchoring banks in the past could condemn banks to invest solely in the riskiest and most illiquid loans such as commercial real estate lending and loans to SMEs?[5] If so, that would undermine rather than promote financial stability.[6]

In sum, Basel is likely to be best, both for banks and for the financial system as a whole. The program to make banks less likely to fail is already proving its worth. Banks have higher capital and more liquidity. The program to make banks safe to fail is on the way to completion. This will make banks more like other firms. Investors, not taxpayers, would bear the cost of failure, and the bank-in-resolution would continue to perform critical economic functions. Banks would become safe to fail as well as less likely to fail. This would enhance financial stability, assure that banks contribute to development and growth and give banks the scope to continue to live in the market.

Notes

Introduction: Resolvability Will Determine the Future of Banking

1. Dewatripont & Tirole (1994, pp. 31–32, 87–92).

1 "Too Big to Fail" Is Too Costly to Continue

1. For a discussion of the impact of financial crises on economic growth, see Huertas (2011a, pp. 1–2) , Rogoff and Reinhart (2009), and BCBS (2010a).
2. On the consequences of Lehmans' failure, see Huertas (2011, pp. 82–83). For an analysis of Lehmans itself, see Valukas (2010).
3. FSB (2013b) lists the 29 G-SIBs. For the criteria describing what makes a bank systemic, see BCBS (2013a). This builds on earlier work, including Tarashev et al. (2009).
4. On the importance of financial market infrastructures, see CPSS-IOSCO (2012).
5. For a discussion of these policy measures, see Huertas (2011, pp. 82–99).
6. Larry Summers used this phrase in his remarks at the IMF Economic Forum on 8 November 2013. See Kose and Portillo (2013).
7. Key factors determining the credit rating of a sovereign are the debt-to-GDP level, the trend in that level and the probability that an event may occur that will require massive additions to government expenditure. One such "event risk" is the possibility that a government might have to rescue one or more of its banks (see Moody's Investor Services, 2013a).
8. Gros (2013) coined the term "doom loop".
9. On forward guidance, see Bernanke (2012), BoE (2013a), Cœuré (2013), and Woodford (2013).
10. On quantitative easing, see Bernanke and Reinhardt (2004), Bernanke (2012), and Joyce et al. (2011).
11. On outstanding level of Fed's holdings of mortgage-backed securities, see Federal Reserve balance sheet week ended 8 January 2014 at http://www.federalreserve.gov/releases/h41/current/h41.htm#h41tab3.

12. For a discussion of ECB monetary policy, see ECB (2012).
13. There are some exceptions to this statement, e.g., the ECB is holding in reserve the actual implementation of its "outright monetary transactions" policy (the direct purchase of government bonds).
14. G-20 (2009).
15. Information on FSOC is available at http://www.treasury.gov/Pages/default.aspx, on the ESRB at http://www.esrb.europa.eu/home/html/index.en.html, and on the FPC at http://www.bankofengland.co.uk/financialstability/pages/fpc/default.aspx.
16. See Tucker (2012) and Moody's Investor Services (2013a).
17. On Eurozone, see also Merler and Pisani-Ferry (2012), and Huertas (2013a).
18. See Moody's Investor Services (2013b).
19. Haldane (2010, p. 25) estimated the subsidy to global banks to be approximately $40 billion in 2007 prior to the crisis, but $250 billion in 2009. See also Schlich et al., 2014.
20. Cunliffe (2014). See also Powell (2013), and Lew (2013).

2   Less Likely to Fail: Strengthening Regulation

1. For full details, see BCBS (2011a, b). BCBS (2011c) provides a summary template and guidelines regarding disclosure.
2. In addition to the items discussed in the text, Basel III requires banks to deduct the following from CET1 capital amounts relating to (i) its cash flow hedge reserve, (ii) the shortfall of the stock of provisions to expected losses, (iii) the gain on sale related to securitisation transactions, (iv) investments in own shares, (v) cumulative gains and losses due to changes in own credit risk on fair valued financial liabilities and (vi) reciprocal cross-holdings in the capital of banking, financial and insurance entities. The bank also had to take into account any unfunded pension fund liabilities on its balance sheet when calculating CET1 capital.
3. The rationale in each case was that such assets could not readily and unequivocally absorb loss. In the case of deferred tax assets, they could not be readily sold to third parties and their value hinges upon the bank actually earning a profit in the future. Consequently, banks have to deduct deferred tax assets in full from CET1 capital, but may put DTAs relating to timing differences into the sin bucket. In the case of mortgage servicing rights, they could be sold to third parties, but their value realised might deviate markedly from book value, especially if interest rates were to change and/or a large number of

institutions were to attempt to sell such rights at the same time.In the case of investments in other financial institutions, the intent was to restrict the extent to which capital could be double counted within the banking system as a whole. The actual limits depend on the degree of control that the investing bank might have over the investee financial institution, as measured by the share of the investing bank's interest in the common equity of the investee institution. For small interests (ownership interest less than 10 per cent), the investing bank is able to hold positions in aggregate of up to 10 per cent of its own CET1 capital. Any amount in excess of this threshold has to be deducted from CET1 capital in full. For significant ownership interests in unconsolidated financial institutions (ownership interest greater than 10 per cent) the investing bank has to deduct the entire amount of its holdings in the common stock of the investee bank (but this amount can be put into the sin bucket).

4. Regarding the capital conservation buffer, see BCBS (2011a, pp. 54–57).

5. On the systemic surcharge, see BCBS (2013a).

6. On the counter-cyclical capital buffer, see BCBS (2010c) and (2011a, pp. 5–7, 57–60). For an analysis, see Drehmann et al. (2010) and Repullo and Saurina (2011).

7. For the trading book, see BCBS (2011d). For the securitisation framework, see BCBS (2013c).

8. BCBS (2011a, pp. 3, 29–51).

9. BCBS (2013d).

10. For the banking book, see BCBS (2013e). For the trading book, see BCBS (2013f).

11. Basel III introduced the leverage ratio in concept in 2010 (see BCBS, 2011a, pp. 4–5, 60–64) and has progressively refined the approach (BCBS, 2013i). In January 2014 the committee reached a final decision on the definition of the ratio (BCBS, 2014a).

12. BoE (2013b, pp. 69–70).

13. BCBS (2014a).

14. Ibid.

15. BoE (2013b, pp. 69–70) also documents differences in the leverage ratio according to the measurement standard employed, as does UST et al. (2013).

16. PRA (2013a) gives details. The 3 per cent ratio corresponds to the definition in the EU Capital Requirements Regulation (CRR).

17. For a discussion of the Bank of England's views on leverage, see BoE (2013b, p. 69). In a letter to the Governor of the Bank of England the Chancellor of the Exchequer (HMT, 2013a) stresses that the PRA

already has the power to set leverage ratios for individual banks and for the system as a whole and that the FPC has the power to make recommendations to the PRA in this respect. The Chancellor also asked the Bank to consider whether the FPC should be granted the authority to set the leverage ratio directly rather than merely recommend to the PRA the steps that the PRA should take.

18. UST et al. (2013). The US proposal refers to the original Basel III agreement (BCBS, 2011a) with respect to leverage rather than the revised (BCBS, 2013i) or final (BCBS, 2014a) proposal. However, the US proposal indicates that the United States will adapt the proposal to conform to changes that the Basel Committee may make in the global approach.

19. FSB 2014a.

20. BCBS (2008a) details the principles for liquidity risk management and supervision. The original Basel III accord (BCBS, 2011a) introduced the concept of a global liquidity standard. Subsequent work has refined the components relating to the liquidity coverage ratio (BCBS, 2013b, 2014b) and its disclosure to supervisors and the public (BCBS, 2014c). The Committee has also further developed the concept of a net stable funding ratio (BCBS, 2014d).

21. This avoids what Goodhart (2010, p. 175) has called the "taxi-rank" problem – a requirement that one taxi always be waiting at the train station, with the result that it cannot be used until a second taxi arrives.

22. BCBS (2010b, pp. 25–31, 2014d).

23. This section draws on EY (2013a). FSB (2013a) states the overall policy and is the source of the quotes in this section.

24. For details, see BCBS (2013g).

25. On remuneration reform, see FSF (2009); and FSB (2009). FSB (2011b) provides an overview of how jurisdictions have implemented the principles. See also Huertas (2011, pp. 171–172).

26. FSB (2013c, pp. 26–28) provides a summary. For details on progress, see FSB (2013d).

27. For an assessment of benefits, see BIS (2013).

28. For a summary of authorities' efforts to coordinate their approaches, see ODRG (2013)

29. In December 2013 the CFTC, the US agency responsible for the regulation of derivatives, outlined its view on the comparability of derivatives regimes in six foreign jurisdictions to US rules as part of its program of substituted compliance (with US rules). In other words, the CFTC view of coordination is the process by which others comply with the CFTC's rules, not to the degree to which US and other regimes satisfy global standards. For details, see CFTC (2013).

30. For a summary of the swaps push out rule, see Nazareth (2013).
31. For UK legislation, see United Kingdom (2013). The paper introducing the draft bill (HMT/BIS 2013) contains the rationale for the legislation. This is largely based a report by the Independent Commission on Banking (2011) chaired by John Vickers. Note however that the original ICB report recognised that retail banking could be as risky as investment banking.
32. Liikanen (2012a). For the full report, see Liikanen (2012b). The French Law of 26 July 2013 is available at http://www.legifrance. gouv.fr/affichTexte.do?cidTexte=JORFTEXT000027754539. For the German law, see http://www.bundesrat.de/cln_330/SharedDocs/ Drucksachen/2013/0301–400/378–13,templateId=raw,property=pub licationFile.pdf/378–13.pdf.
33. The final Volcker Rule is a joint rule of the five US federal agencies responsible for regulation and supervision of financial institutions in the United States (Board of Governors of the Federal Reserve System, Office of the Comptroller of the Currency, Federal Deposit Insurance Corporation, Securities and Exchange Commission and Commodities Futures Trading Corporation). The final text of the rule is available at http://www.federalreserve.gov/newsevents/press/ bcreg/bcreg20131210a1.pdf. For a summary and legal analysis, see S&S (2014).
34. The rule also applies to non-US banking organisations. Their US operations are subject to the rule in the same manner as US banking organisations, and their non-US operations are also subject to the rule unless such operations are "solely outside the United States." Note that the rule classifies trading with a US person outside the United States as being "within the United States" so that foreign banking organisations that trade with US persons (such as US banks) in covered financial instruments will effectively become subject to very extensive US reporting and compliance requirements.
35. On balkanisation, see Goodhart (2013, pp. 254–255).
36. HMT (2012, pp. 7–8).
37. See FINMA (2012).
38. Tarullo (2012).
39. FRB (2012) and FRB 2014.
40. Barker and Braithwaite (2013).
41. For a general discussion of financial institution taxation in the wake of the crisis, see IMF (2010).
42. For an economic analysis of the FTT, see Matheson (2011).
43. A summary of developments with respect to the EU proposal for a FTT is available at http://ec.europa.eu/taxation_customs/taxation/ other_taxes/financial_sector/index_En.htm.

44. See Perotti and Suarez (2011).

3 *Less Likely to Fail: Sharper Supervision*

1. On micro-supervision, see Sants (2009); Huertas (2011, pp. 184–192); and PRA (2013b).
2. For example, the German supervisor BAFIN rejected Deutsche Bank's first choice for chief risk officer. See Taylor and Hübner (2012).
3. See, e.g., PRA (2013b, p. 17).
4. Quote is from Sants (2009).
5. FSB 2014b.
6. BCBS (2013h).
7. The United Kingdom is one example. See PRA (2013b, pp. 30–31).
8. For the US rule on capital plans, see FRB (2011). Note that the supervisory review of the bank's capital plan will also have a macro-prudential dimension, especially in the case where the bank is systemically significant in the domestic economy. Although reductions in the growth or absolute level of assets is one way to improve a bank's capital ratio, the supervisor is hardly likely to approve such plans if they involve a reduction in credit to SMEs and households at the trough of the cycle.
9. PRA (2013b, p. 26).
10. The United States conducts an annual comprehensive capital assessment review (CCAR) (see FRB, 2011). The EU conducts a stress test periodically for all EU banks. This will be coordinated with the asset quality review to be conducted by the ECB for Eurozone banks. Individual jurisdictions within the EU also conduct stress tests (for the United Kingdom, see PRA, 2013b, p. 26; BoE, 2013d).
11. For details of the ECB asset quality review, see Constâncio (2013) and Huertas (2013a).
12. The principles are detailed in BCBS (2008a).
13. BCBS (2013j) details the behaviour under stress of various funding sources including the implications for unencumbered assets. It also provides a survey of the academic literature relating to these issues. See also BoE (2013d).
14. For details of central bank lending policies in the United States, see FRB (2010) and Board of Governors of the Federal Reserve System (2013); in the United Kingdom, see BoE (2013c); and in the Eurozone, see ECB (2011).
15. On recovery planning, see Huertas and Lastra (2011); PRA (2013c); EBA (2013).

16. For a discussion of supervisory intervention, see PRA (2013b, pp. 30–35).
17. For a summary of history of FSB, see http://www.financialstability-board.org/about/history.htm.
18. For an example of such a periodic report, see FSB (2013c) and FSB 2014a.
19. For background on the Financial Stability Oversight Council, see http://www.treasury.gov/initiatives/fsoc/about/Pages/default.aspx.
20. For background on the ESRB, see http://www.esrb.europa.eu/about/background/html/index.en.html.
21. For background on the FPC, see http://www.bankofengland.co.uk/financialstability/pages/fpc/default.aspx.
22. The so-called credit view of the monetary transmission mechanism contends that the availability and volume of bank credit has an independent effect on the aggregate economic variables such as consumption and investment over and above the impact from interest rates alone. Hence, if bank capital or bank liquidity constrains (facilitates) bank lending, movements in bank capital and/or liquidity will augment the cycle. See Bolton and Freixas (2006). Brunnermeier et al. (2009) document that movements in asset prices will have a pro-cyclical effect on capital (via market-to-market accounting) and on liquidity (via valuation of and advance rates on collateral used in repos and other secured borrowings). This creates a positive feedback loop, augmenting the upturn and deepening the downturn. See also Huertas (2011a, p. 41).
23. For details of the counter-cyclical capital buffer, see BCBS (2010c). On the effectiveness of the buffer in offsetting pro-cyclicality, see Repullo and Saurina (2011).
24. On debt overhang, see Admati et al. (2012).
25. For details of the AQR/BSA that the ECB proposes to conduct in connection with the introduction of banking union, see ECB (2013a) and Huertas (2013a).
26. See FSB (2013f). For a general discussion of shadow banking, see Poszar et al. (2013); Kodres (2013); Tarullo (2013); Jackson (2013); Huertas (2011a, pp. 206–210).
27. On "acquire to arbitrage," see Huertas (2011a, pp. 35–38).
28. In the United States the FSOC (2012) made proposals to this effect in November 2012 as did the European Commission (2013) in September 2013.
29. For the FSB recommendation, see FSB (2013g).
30. For an analysis of re-hypothecation, see Singh and Aitken (2010).
31. On risks in the repo market and proposed mitigation, see FSB (2013g); Dudley (2013); FRBNY (2012); FSOC (2012, p. 133).

32. The over-reliance on intraday credit results from the decision of the two hub banks to act in effect as principal rather than agent in the tri-party market. They have tended to repay the lenders (repurchase the securities) at the start of business each day without demanding repayment from the borrower (e.g., a broker-dealer) in the expectation that the borrower would be able to find a new third-party lender by the close of the business day. During the day the hub bank acts as the lender to the borrower. This creates undue concentration risk:
    - for major broker-dealers and other firms that rely on repo for the bulk of their short-term funding. If the hub bank decides to increase collateral demands (haircuts) or cut off credit entirely, this could push the broker-dealer into resolution – a step that could have system-wide repercussions.
    - or the system as a whole, if one or both of the hub banks were to fail, so might many of the borrowers, for they would be hard-pressed to make immediately alternative funding arrangements.

    This risk is being addressed. The hub banks are revising their clearing arrangements to reduce the intraday credit that they provide. By year end 2014 approximately 90 per cent of tri-party repo will be on an agency basis where the loan comes directly to the borrower from the lender without any intra-day credit from the hub bank. See Dudley (2013).
33. For example, lenders have set haircuts too low relative to the risk of the borrower and the price volatility and market liquidity of the collateral. Lenders have also taken as collateral securities that they would not be allowed to own outright.
34. Lenders generally do not have a mechanism in place to allow for gradual liquidation of collateral seized in the event a borrower defaults. Lenders therefore attempt to sell immediately the assets taken in lieu of repayment. In the event of a default by a major broker-dealer, dumping very large amounts of securities into an already troubled market will depress prices to "fire sale" levels and cause further mark-downs in capital and shortages in liquidity in various participants across the market as a whole.
35. In the United States, e.g., the Financial Stability Oversight Committee has formally designated nine financial market infrastructures as systemically important financial market utilities. See http://www.treasury.gov/initiatives/fsoc/Documents/2012%20Appendix%20A%20Designation%20of%20Systemically%20Important%20Market%20Utilities.pdf.
36. See CPSS-IOSCO (2012).
37. For recovery plans, see CPSS-IOSCO (2013). For resolution plans for FMIs, see FSB (2013e, pp. 15–26) and Huertas 2014a.

38. FSB (2013c, p. 16).
39. FSB (2013h). In the United States the FSOC has designated American International Group and Prudential Financial as systemically important financial institutions (see http://www.treasury.gov/initiatives/fsoc/designations/Pages/default.aspx).
40. The exception to this statement is General Electric Capital Corporation, which the FSOC designated as systemic in July 2013 (FSOC, 2013a).
41. On Fannie and Freddie, see Acharya et al. (2011) and Huertas (2011a, pp. 209–210).
42. In addition, a number of banks "low-balled" their LIBOR submissions during the crisis in order to avoid giving the appearance that they were under liquidity pressure and had to pay up for funds. In at least one case (Barclays) it appeared that this was done with the knowledge and approval of the bank's senior management. When this came to light, the senior management of the bank was replaced. Cf. CFTC (2012).
43. Wheatley (2012).
44. IOSCO (2013).
45. Griffin and Campbell (2013).
46. For an overview of securitisation, see Jackson (2013, pp. 383–392).
47. Huertas (2011a, pp. 29–33) and Jackson (2013).
48. On reform of credit rating agencies, see FSB (2013c, pp. 30–32).
49. For a list of prominent SEC enforcement cases with respect to insider trading, see http://www.sec.gov/spotlight/insidertrading/cases.shtml.
50. Financial Action Task Force (2012).
51. On initiatives with respect to consumer protection, see OECD (2013) and FSB (2011a).
52. For further information on the CFPB, see http://www.consumerfinance.gov/.
53. FCA (2013, pp. 10–24).
54. Indeed, prior to the crisis central banks and other authorities remained quite optimistic about the economy, stating that growth would continue and that there was little or no chance of a recession developing – all thanks to the "Great Moderation" that central bank monetary policy had helped bring about (Bernanke, 2004). Consequently, in normal times the economy is as or more likely to drive the supply of credit as credit supply is likely to drive the economy.

4   *Safe to Fail*

1. FSB (2011c).

2. Normal transactions would include payments and settlement of securities trades and various other "non-investment" transactions with both individual and institutional customers. In contrast, investment obligations would be subject to a stay (e.g., on the payment of interest and dividends or the repayment of capital instruments) as outlined later.

3. For a description of the key attributes of a resolution regime, see FSB (2011c). For an assessment of progress in implementation of these key attributes, see FSB (2013i, j).

4. For details, see Huertas (2014b) ; Huertas and Nieto (2014).

5. In some jurisdictions the central bank has a formal role in the trigger process. For example, in the United Kingdom under the Banking Act 2009 the Financial Services Authority (the supervisor at the time) had to seek the advice of the Bank of England before formally pulling the trigger (finding that the bank failed to meet threshold conditions).

6. However, the supervisor alone can exercise forbearance, if the bank finances itself solely through equity and insured deposits. This occurred in the United States in the 1980s in the case of savings and loan associations (thrifts). In many ways, the "prompt corrective action" provisions of FDICIA (1991) were designed to put a limit on such supervisory forbearance.

7. However, forbearance and the provision of emergency liquidity assistance does give unsecured creditors both the opportunity and incentive to run and get out whole (without loss) before the bank enters resolution. To keep the bank in operation, the central bank would have to extend increasing amounts of collateralised credit, further reducing the unencumbered assets that might serve to back the bank's unsecured liabilities and furthering increasing the losses that such creditors would suffer, if the bank eventually did enter resolution.

8. Such disruption from closing an internationally active bank in the middle of the day is known as "Herstatt risk." This refers principally to settlement risk – the risk that one side of a transaction will settle, whilst the other remains open. Although infrastructures and participants have taken various measures to reduce such risks, significant settlement risks remain. In addition, closing a G-SIB in the middle of a business day is likely to cause a significant number of trades to fail. This may have knock-on effects on the risk positions of major market participants. See Huertas (2014a).

9. See FSB (2013j) and FSB 2014a.

10. Conceptually, it is possible to set in advance the terms on which write-off or conversion would occur, if the bank went into resolution.

To the extent that investor obligations contain such clauses, the resolution authority should implement them immediately at or immediately before putting the bank into resolution. The converted instrument would then slot into the creditor hierarchy in its new capacity.

Conceptually, it is also possible to imagine that the resolution authority would set the terms of conversion at the resolution weekend, or that the terms could be negotiated among the parties during the weekend. The former is potentially arbitrary, so that it will be more difficult for the bank to place instruments with investors. The latter is utterly impractical, given the short time period available (36–48 hours), the diversity of investor interests and the inability to establish with precision the amount of loss that the bank must take.

11. Note that it may not be necessary to bail-in the senior debt, if the amount of Additional Tier 1 and Tier 2 capital is sufficient to recapitalise the bank.

12. Note that the issuance of such proceeds notes greatly reduces the need to conduct an immediate valuation of the bank-in-resolution for the purpose of apportioning ultimate loss. Provided the authorities do not engage in forbearance (allow banks that fail to meet threshold conditions to continue in operation), losses should be less than the amount of the bank's primary loss-absorbing capacity (common equity plus instruments subject to mandatory bail-in). Consequently, the valuation immediately required at the point of resolution is
    - an assessment that the bank has reached the point of non-viability (so that the trigger to resolution is pulled);
    - an assessment that losses will not be greater than the total amount of investor capital (primary loss absorbing capacity); and
    - an assessment of the advance rate that the central bank is willing to make on the unencumbered assets that the bank-in-resolution will pledge to the central bank as collateral for the liquidity facility that the central bank provides to the bank-in-resolution.

13. IIF (2011). However, some resolution regimes (e.g., EU BRRD) leave open how such a claim could be satisfied.

14. On asset encumbrance, see CGFS (2013).

15. See Huertas (2014a).

16. For a discussion of the impact of QFCs on resolution, see Roe (2011).

17. Huertas (2013a).

18. See Bovenzi et al. (2013).

19. For example, Iceland changed its banking law in 2008 after the entry in resolution of Landsbanki and other Icelandic banks with foreign branches.

20. See, e.g., PRA (2014).
21. FDIC (2013).
22. In the United States, e.g., the FDIC may employ the Orderly Liquidation Authority (the basis for the SPE approach) if and only if it can demonstrate that resolution under normal bankruptcy procedures (as called for under Title I) would be harmful to financial stability in the United States and this decision has the prior approval of the FDIC itself (two-thirds of its board), the Board of Governors of the Federal Reserve System (with two-thirds majority) and the Secretary of the Treasury "in consultation with the President."
23. FDIC (2013).
24. FRB (2014).
25. In particular, such a process shall make clear that the original parent holding company has no claim on the subsidiary bank-in-resolution, but mandate that the original parent holding company provide a warranty and indemnity to the restructured bank-in-resolution for liabilities relating to misconduct at the subsidiary bank-in-resolution prior to the entry of the subsidiary bank into resolution. Note that condition (2) (the restriction on the parent holding company paying dividends or making distributions) holds only so long as the parent owns the subsidiary. If the subsidiary enters resolution and the parent's equity is written off, the parent is no longer responsible for assuring that the bank-in-resolution has adequate reserve capital.
26. For further discussion of such a liquidity facility see Huertas (2013a).
27. Merton and Perold (1993). See also Strongin (2013).

5 Setting Up for Success

1. For a discussion of supervisors as monitors and minders, see Huertas (2012b).
2. To a certain extent, investors can supplement their own analysis of the bank by "free-riding" on the supervisor's monitoring and minding activities. The supervisor will generally have greater power than a private investor to obtain information from the bank. To the extent that such regulatory reports are made public in a timely manner, investors can get sight of the same data that the supervisor uses to judge the bank's condition. This will aid investors in forming their own view of the bank's condition.

   The supervisor will also generally have more power to "persuade" the bank to take the measures necessary to arrest deterioration in its condition and/or to initiate its recovery plan. What investors will do is form a view on effectiveness of the supervisor as a "minder": can the supervisor identify problems promptly, can it induce the bank to take remedial measures as soon as possible and can it refrain from exercising forbearance? If so, this "minding" activity will reduce the probability that the bank will reach the point of non-viability/enter resolution as well as reduce the loss to investors, if the bank does enter resolution.

3. Low RoE-low risk equities can perform just as well or better than high RoE-high risk equities. In fact, total return to shareholders from holding utility stocks (a proxy for low return-low risk equities) has compared favourably with the total return realised by shareholders in financial institutions. See Huertas (2009).

4. This, of course, is just a restatement of textbook corporate finance, the so-called Modigliani-Miller theorem. Under too big to fail, banks have been largely exempt from the rule that higher risk means a higher cost of equity capital. Resolution reform will remove that exemption and make banks more similar to non-financial corporations. For further discussion see Huertas (2012b, 2013c).

5. Secondarily, the bank may earn income from the instruments whilst they are in inventory.

6. At a minimum, the business model should include all the risks the bank will take. Had such an analysis been conducted prior to the crisis, banks might have seen that they were overlooking or underestimating liquidity risk as well as conduct and operational risks.

7. The business model should assure that the bank prices risk correctly. Under-charging customers for the risk of credit is particularly dangerous. Banks that follow such a policy will gain a disproportionate share of such credit and fail to earn enough income over time to provision adequately for the impairments that will arise.

8. For example, if a bank is to compete in offering credit cards to consumers, it has to be ready to offer customers limits that are in line with the income and spending habits of its target customer base.

9. Acemoglu and Robinson (2012).

10. Quote is from Sands (2013). In fact, finance has a long history of such moments – the negotiable CD, money market mutual funds, derivatives and so on; so it will pay banks to think through how markets may evolve and to be prepared to adopt and/or adapt innovations that may occur elsewhere.

11. Although regulation may currently provide some protection against competition from new entrants, banks should not derive too much comfort from this. Any benefit is likely to be temporary. The prospect of profit makes potential entrants quite inventive in devising ways to

access the most profitable parts of the revenue pool. And the prospect of lower prices and/or better service, along with the view that small firms do not pose a threat to financial stability, may persuade the authorities to tolerate or even welcome the additional competition that new entrants would pose.

12. There are already examples of banks moving in this direction. See Chassany and Goff (2014).
13. See Huertas (2011, pp. 35–38); Jackson (2013).
14. This should be documented in the bank's risk appetite framework and risk appetite statement – each of which will be subject to supervisory review (see Chapter 2).
15. For a fuller description of the role of internal audit, see Chartered Institute of Internal Auditors (2013).
16. Banks purportedly pursued this strategy prior to the crisis. Actually, they didn't. They failed to distribute. Assets got stuck on the bank's balance sheet, so that the strategy in practice became "acquire to arbitrage" rather than originate to distribute. See Huertas (2011, pp. 35–38).
17. On acquire-to-arbitrage, see ibid.
18. In some cases, holding "idle" inventory may actually detract from the bank's ability to win new business. For example, if a bank's existing loans to a corporate client already approach its internal or legal lending limit, the bank will have little or no scope to respond to new credit demands from the client.
19. See McGrath (2013).
20. See Mayer-Schönberger and Cukier (2013); Davenport (2013); Davenport and Harris (2010).

Conclusion: Is Basel Best?

1. In addition, as outlined in Chapter 4, banks and authorities will have to develop a means to assure that qualified financial contracts do not disrupt the resolution process as well as a means to assure that financial market infrastructures remain robust.
2. It will certainly help, as outlined in Chapter 5, if banks can devise means to make work to meet regulatory requirements do "double duty" and meet business requirements as well.
3. See Powell (2013), for example.
4. In an extreme case, global banks would become little more than owners of various national entities, each independent of one another. This could hamper trade and growth, particularly if such national

entities could not readily book business with institutions or individuals resident outside the borders of the country in which the bank is incorporated.

5. Goodhart (2013, p. 15).

6. The US savings and loan (thrift) industry is a good example of the unintended adverse consequences of financial regulation. Regulation forced such banks to specialise in long-term, fixed rate mortgages financed by short-term insured deposits subject to a ceiling (Regulation Q) on the rate of interest that could be paid to depositors. When the Federal Reserve raised interest rates above the Reg Q ceiling in order to combat inflation, thrifts experienced significant deposit outflows, leading to the failure of over one thousand thrifts, the collapse of its deposit insurance fund and a bill to the taxpayer of over $150 billion. For a summary, see White (1991).

Bibliography

Acemoglu, D., and Robinson, J. (2012). *Why Nations Fail: The Origins of Power, Prosperity, and Poverty*. New York: Crown Publishers.

Acharya, V. V., Richardson, M., van Nieuwerburgh, S., & White, L. (2011). *Guaranteed to Fail: Fannie Mac, Freddie Mac, and the Debacle of Mortgage Finance*. Princeton: Princeton University Press.

Admati, A. R., De Marzo, P. M., Hellwig, M. F., & Pfleiderer, P. (2012). *Debt Overhang and Capital Regulation*. Rock Center for Corporate Governance Working Paper 114. Retrieved December 2013, from: http://ssrn.com/abstract=2031204.

Bank of England. (BoE; 2013a). *Monetary Policy Trade-Offs and Forward Guidance*. Retrieved December 2013, from: http://www.bankofengland.co.uk/publications/Documents/inflationreport/2013/ir13augforwardguidance.pdf.

——— (2013b). *Financial Stability Report*. Retrieved December 2013, from: http://www.bankofengland.co.uk/publications/Documents/fsr/2013/fsr34sec5.pdf.

——— (2013c). *The Bank of England's Sterling Money Market Framework ("Red Book")*. Retrieved December 2013, from: http://www.bankofengland.co.uk/markets/Documents/money/publications/redbook.pdf.

——— (2013d). *A Framework for Stress Testing the UK Banking System*. Retrieved December 2013, from: http://www.bankofengland.co.uk/financialstability/fsc/Documents/discussionpaper1013.pdf.

Bank for International Settlements. (BIS; 2013). Macroeconomic assessment group on derivatives. *Macroeconomic Impact Assessment of OTC Derivatives Regulatory Reforms*. Retrieved December 2013, from: http://www.bis.org/publ/othp20.pdf.

Barker, A., & Braithwaite, T. (2013, April 22). *EU Warns US on "Bank Protectionism."* Retrieved December 2013, from: http://web.xrh.unipi.gr/attachments/370_EU%20warns%20US%20on%20bank.pdf.

Basel Committee on Banking Supervision. (BCBS; 2008a). Basel Committee on Banking Supervision. *Principles for Sound Liquidity Risk Management and Supervision*. Retrieved from: http://www.bis.org/publ/bcbs144.pdf.

——— (2008b). Basel Committee on Banking Supervision. *External Audit Quality and Banking Supervision*. Retrieved from: http://www.bis.org/publ/bcbs146.pdf.

———— (2010a). *Basel III: International Framework for Liquidity Risk Measurement, Standards and Monitoring.* Retrieved December 2013, from: http://www.bis.org/publ/bcbs188.pdf .

———— (2010b). *An Assessment of the Long-Term Impact of Stronger Capital and Liquidity Requirements.* Retrieved from: http://www.bis.org/publ/bcbs173.pdf.

———— (2010c). *Guidance for National Authorities Operating the Countercyclical Capital Buffer.* Retrieved December 2013, from: http://www.bis.org/publ/bcbs187.pdf.

———— (2011a). *Basel III: A Global Regulatory Framework for More Resilient Banks and Banking Systems.* Retrieved December 2013, from: http://www.bis.org/publ/bcbs211.pdf.

———— (2011b). *Basel III Definition of Capital – Frequently Asked Questions.* Retrieved December 2013, from: http://www.bis.org/publ/bcbs211.pdf.

———— (2011c). *Definition of Capital Disclosure Requirements.* Retrieved December 2013, from: http://www.bis.org/publ/bcbs212.pdf.

———— (2011d). *Revisions to the Basel II Market Risk Framework.* Retrieved December 2013, from: http://www.bis.org/publ/bcbs193.pdf.

———— (2013a). *Global Systemically Important Banks: Updated Assessment Methodology and the Higher Loss Absorbency Requirement.* Retrieved December 2013, from: http://www.bis.org/publ/bcbs255.pdf.

———— (2013b). *Basel III: The Liquidity Coverage Ratio and Liquidity Risk Monitoring Tools.* Retrieved December 2013, from: http://www.bis.org/publ/bcbs238.pdf.

———— (2013c) *Revisions to the Securitisation Framework: Consultative Document.* Retrieved December 2013, from: https://www.bis.org/publ/bcbs269.pdf.

———— (2013d). *Fundamental Review of the Trading Book: A Revised Market Risk Framework.* Retrieved December 2013, from: https://www.bis.org/publ/bcbs265.pdf.

———— (2013e). *Regulatory Consistency Assessment Programme (RCAP) Analysis of Risk-Weighted Assets for Credit Risk in the Banking Book.* Retrieved December 2013, from: http://www.bis.org/publ/bcbs256.pdf.

———— (2013f). *Regulatory Consistency Assessment Programme (RCAP) Analysis of Risk-Weighted Assets for Market Risk.* Retrieved December 2013, from: http://www.bis.org/publ/bcbs240.pdf.

———— (2013g). *Principles for Effective Risk Data Aggregation and Risk Reporting.* Retrieved December 2013, from: http://www.bis.org/publ/bcbs239.pdf.

———— (2013h). *External Audits of Banks. Consultative Document.* Retrieved December 2013, from: http://www.bis.org/publ/bcbs244.pdf.

———— (2013i). *Revised Basel III Leverage Ratio Framework and Disclosure Requirements. Consultation Document.* Retrieved from: https://www.bis.org/publ/bcbs251.pdf.

———— (2013j). *Liquidity Stress Testing: A Survey of Theory, Empirics and Current Industry and Supervisory Practices.* Retrieved December 2013, from Working Paper 24: http://www.bis.org/publ/bcbs_wp24.pdf.

———— (2014a). *Basel III Leverage Ratio Framework and Disclosure Requirements.* Retrieved January 2014, from: https://www.bis.org/publ/bcbs270.pdf.

———— (2014b). *Revisions to Basel III: The Liquidity Coverage Ratio and Liquidity Risk Monitoring Tools (January 2013).* Retrieved January 2014, from: http://www.bis.org/publ/bcbs274.pdf.

———— (2014c). *Liquidity Coverage Ratio Disclosure Standards.* Retrieved January 2014, from: http://www.bis.org/publ/bcbs272.pdf.

———— (2014d). *Basel III: The Net Stable Funding Ratio: Consultative Document.* Retrieved January 2014, from: http://www.bis.org/publ/bcbs271.pdf.

Bernanke, B. S. (2004). *The Great Moderation.* Remarks before the Eastern Economic Association February 20, 2004. Retrieved December 2013, from: http://www.federalreserve.gov/Boarddocs/Speeches/2004/20040220/.

————. (2012). *Monetary Policy since the Onset of the Crisis.* Retrieved December 2013, from: http://www.federalreserve.gov/newsevents/speech/bernanke20120831a.pdf.

Bernanke, B. S., & Reinhart, V. (2004). Conducting Monetary Policy at Very Low Short-Term Interest Rates. *American Economic Review, 94*(2), 85–90.

Bolton, P., & Freixas, X. (2006). Corporate Finance and the Monetary Transmission Mechanism. *Review of Financial Studies, 19,* 829–870.

Bovenzi, J., Guynn, R. D., & Jackson, T. H. (2013, May). *Too Big to Fail: The Path to a Solution. A Report of the Failure Resolution Task Force of the Financial Regulatory Reform Initiative of the Bipartisan Policy Center.* Retrieved January 2014, from: http://bipartisanpolicy.org/sites/default/files/TooBigToFail.pdf.

Brunnermeier, M., Crockett, A., Goodhart, C., Persaud, A. D., & Shin, H. (2009). *The Fundamental Principles of Financial Regulation. Geneva Reports on the World Economy 11.* Geneva: International Center for Monetary and Banking Studies.

Chartered Institute of Internal Auditors. (2013). *Effective Internal Audit in the Financial Services Sector: Recommendations from the Committee on Internal Audit Guidance for the Financial Sector.* Retrieved January 2014, from: http://www.iia.org.uk/media/354788/0758_Effective_internal_audit_financial_webfinal.pdf.

Chassany, A.-S., & Goff, S. (2014). Barclays Joins Forces with BlueBay to Bolster Riskier Lending. *Financial Times*, 9 January 2014. Retrieved January 2014, from: http://www.ft.com/intl/cms/s/0/445b5f56–7884 –11e3–831c-00144feabdc0.html#axzz2qZfWGmTi.

Čihák, M., Demirgüç-Kunt, A., Feyen, E., & Levine, R. (2013). Financial Development in 205 Economies, 1960 to 2010. *Journal of Financial Persepctives, 1*(2), 17–35.

Cœuré, B. (2013, September). *The Usefulness of Forward Guidance.* Retrieved December 2013, from: http://www.ecb.europa.eu/press/key/date/2013/html/sp130926_1.en.html.

Committee on the Global Financial System. (CGFS; 2013). *Asset Encumbrance, Financial Reform and the Demand for Collateral Assets.* Retrieved December 2013, from: http://www.bis.org/publ/cgfs49.pdf.

Committee on Payment and Settlement Systems and Technical Committee of the International Organisation of Securities Commissions. (2012, April). *Principles for Financial Market Infrastructures.* Retrieved 16 July 2012, from: http://www.bis.org/publ/cpss101a.pdf.

Committee on Payments and Securities Settlement Systems and Board of the International Organisation of Securities Commissions. (2013, August). *Recovery of Financial Market Infrastructures.* Retrieved December 2013, from: http://www.bis.org/publ/cpss109.pdf.

Commodities Futures Trading Corporation. (2012, June 27). *US CFTC Order against Barclays PLC, Barclays Bank PLC and Barclays Capital Inc.* Retrieved December 2013, from: http://www.cftc.gov/ucm/groups/public/@lrenforcementactions/documents/legalpleading/enfbarclaysorder062712.pdf.

———. (2013, December 20). *CFTC Approves Comparability Determinations for Six Jurisdictions for Substituted Compliance Purposes.* Retrieved December 2013, from: http://www.cftc.gov/PressRoom/PressReleases/pr6802–13.

Constâncio, V. (2013). *Banking Union and the Future of Banking.* Retrieved January 2014, from: https://www.bis.org/review/r131203b.pdf.

Cunliffe, J. (2014). *Is the World Financial System Safer Now?* Retrieved from: http://www.bankofengland.co.uk/publications/Documents/speeches/2014/speech714.pdf.

Davenport, T. H. (2013). Analytics 3.0. *Harvard Business Review* (December), 65–72.

Davenport, T., & Harris, J. (2010). *Analytics at Work: Smarter Decisions, Better Results.* Cambridge, MA: Harvard Business Press.

Dewatripont, M., & Tirole, J. (1994). *The Prudential Regulation of Banks.* Cambridge, MA: MIT Press.

Drehmann, M., Borio, C., Gambacorta, L., Jimenez, G., & Trucharte, C. (2010, July). *Countercyclical Capital Buffers: Exploring Options*. Retrieved December 2013, from BIS Working Papers 317: http://www.bis.org/publ/work317.pdf.

Dudley, W. C. (2013, October 4). *Introductory Remarks at Workshop on "Fire Sales" as a Driver of Systemic Risk in Tri-Party Repo and Other Secured Funding Markets*. Retrieved December 2013, from: http://www.newyorkfed.org/newsevents/speeches/2013/dud131004.html.

Ernst & Young. (2013). *GRN Executive Brief: Controlling Risk Appetite*. Retrieved April 2014, from: http://www.ey.com/Publication/vwLU-Assets/EY_Building_Effective_risk_appetite_frameworks/$FILE/EY-Global-Regulatory-Network-Controlling-Risk-Appetite.pdf.

European Banking Authority. (2013). *On the Content of Recovery Plans under the Draft Directive Establishing a Framework for the Recovery and Resolution of Credit Institutions and Investment Firms (EBA/CP/2013/01)*. Retrieved December 2013, from: http://www.eba.europa.eu/documents/10180/40272/EBA-CP-2013-01-CP-on-draft-RTS-on-Content-of-Recovery-Plans.pdf.

European Central Bank. (2011). *The Monetary Policy of the ECB*. Retrieved December 2013, from: http://www.ecb.europa.eu/pub/pdf/other/monetarypolicy2011en.pdf.

———. (2012). *Annual Report 2012*. Retrieved December 2013, from: http://www.ecb.europa.eu/pub/pdf/annrep/ar2012en.pdf.

———. (2013, October 23). *Note Comprehensive Assessment*. Retrieved December 2013, from: http://www.ecb.europa.eu/pub/pdf/other/notecomprehensiveassessment201310en.pdf.

European Commission. (2013). *Proposal for a Regulation of the European Parliament and of the Council on Money Market Funds COM(2013) 615 Final*. Retrieved December 2013, from: http://eur-lex.europa.eu/LexUriServ/LexUriServ.do?uri=COM:2013:0615:FIN:EN:PDF.

European Union. Council. (2013). *Proposal for a Directive establishing a framework for the recovery and resolution of credit institutions and investment firms (BRRD) final compromise text Interinstitutional File: 2012/0150 (COD)*. Retrieved April 2014, from: http://www.plesner.com/resources/934.pdf.

Federal Deposit Insurance Corporation. (FDIC; 2013). *Resolution of Systemically Important Financial Institutions: The Single Point of Entry Strategy*. Retrieved January 2014, from: http://www.gpo.gov/fdsys/pkg/FR-2013-12-18/pdf/2013-30057.pdf.

Federal Reserve Bank of New York, Task Force on Tri-Party Repo Infrastructure Payments Risk Committee. (2012). *Final Report*. Retrieved

December 2013, from: http://www.newyorkfed.org/tripartyrepo/pdf/report_120215.pdf.

Federal Reserve System. (2011). *Capital Plans*. Retrieved December 2013, from:http://www.gpo.gov/fdsys/pkg/FR-2011–12–01/pdf/2011–30665.pdf.

Federal Reserve System Board of Governors. (2010). *Federal Reserve Discount Window*. Retrieved December 2013, from: http://www.frbdiscountwindow.org/discountwindowbook_pf.pdf.

———. (2012, December). *Enhanced Prudential Standards and Early Remediation Requirements for Foreign Banking Organizations and Foreign Nonbank Financial Companies: Proposed Rule*. Retrieved December 2013, from: http://www.gpo.gov/fdsys/pkg/FR-2012–12–28/pdf/2012–30734.pdf.

———. (2013). *Federal Reserve Collateral Guidelines*. Retrieved December 2013,   from: http://www.frbdiscountwindow.org/FRcollguidelines.pdf?hdrID=21&dtlID=81.

———. (2014). *Enhanced Prudential Standards for Bank Holding Companies and Foreign Banking Organizations*. Retrieved April 2014, from: http://www.federalreserve.gov/newsevents/press/bcreg/bcreg20140218a1.pdf.

Financial Action Task Force. (2012). *International Standards on Combating Money Laundering and the Financing of Terrorism and Proliferation: The FATF Recommendations*. Retrieved December 2013, from: http://www.fatf-gafi.org/media/fatf/documents/recommendations/pdfs/FATF_Recommendations.pdf.

Financial Conduct Authority. (2013, July). *The FCA's Approach to Advancing Its Objectives*. Retrieved December 2013, from: http://www.fca.org.uk/static/documents/fca-approach-advancing-objectives.pdf.

Financial Stability Board. (FSB; 2009). *FSB Principles for Sound Compensation Practices: Implementation Standards*. Retrieved December 2013, from: http://www.financialstabilityboard.org/publications/r_090925c.pdf.

———. (2011a). *Consumer Finance Protection with Particular Focus on Credit*. Retrieved December 2013, from: http://www.financialstabilityboard.org/publications/r_111026a.pdf.

———. (2011b). *2011 Thematic Review on Compensation: Peer Review Report*. Retrieved December 2013, from: http://www.financialstabilityboard.org/publications/r_111011a.pdf.

———. (2011c). *Key Attributes of Effective Resolution Regimes for Financial Institutions*. Retrieved May 31, 2012, from: http://www.financialstabilityboard.org/publications/r_111104cc.pdf.

———. (2013a). *Principles for an Effective Risk Appetite Framework*. Retrieved January 2014, from: http://www.financialstabilityboard.org/publications/r_131118.pdf.

———. (2013b). *2013 Update of Group of Global Systemically Important Banks.* Retrieved November 2013, from: http://www.financialstabilityboard. org/publications/r_131111.pdf.

———. (2013c). *Overview of Progress in the Implementation of the G20 Recommendations for Strengthening.* Retrieved December 2013, from: http://www.financialstabilityboard.org/publications/r_130905c.pdf.

———. (2013d). *OTC Derivatives Market Reforms: Sixth Progress Report on Implementation.* Retrieved December 2013, from: http://www.financialstabilityboard.org/publications/r_130902b.pdf.

———. (2013e). *Application of the Key Attributes of Effective Resolution Regimes to Non-Bank Financial Institutions.* Retrieved December 2013, from: http://www.financialstabilityboard.org/publications/r_130812a.pdf.

———. (2013f). *Strengthening Oversight and Regulation of Shadow Banking: An Overview of Policy Recommendations.* Retrieved January 2014, from: http://www.financialstabilityboard.org/publications/r_130829a.pdf.

———. (2013g). *Strengthening Oversight and Regulation of Shadow Banking: Policy Framework for Addressing Shadow Banking Risks in Securities Lending and Repos.* Retrieved January 2014, from: http://www.financialstabilityboard.org/publications/r_130829b.pdf.

———. (2013h). *Global Systemically Important Insurers (G-SIIs) and the Policy Measures That Will Apply to Them.* Retrieved December 2013, from: http://www.financialstabilityboard.org/publications/r_130718.pdf.

———. (2013i). *Thematic Review of Resolution Regimes: Peer Review Report.* Retrieved January 2014, from: http://www.financialstabilityboard.org/publications/r_130411a.pdf.

———. (2013j). *Progress and Next Steps Towards Ending Too Big to Fail: Report of the Financial Stability Board to the G-20.* Retrieved January 2014, from: http://www.financialstabilityboard.org/publications/r_130902.pdf.

———. (2013k). *Thematic Review on Risk Governance: Peer Review Report.* Retrieved May 2013, from: http://www.financialstabilityboard.org/publications/r_130212.pdf.

_____. (2014a). *Financial Reform – Update on Progress.* Retrieved April 2014, from: https://www.financialstabilityboard.org/publications/ r_140411.pdf.

_____. (2014b). *Guidance on Supervisory Interaction with Financial Institutions on Risk Culture:A Framework for Assessing Risk Culture.* Retrieved April 2014 from: https://www.financialstabilityboard.org/ publications/140407.pdf.

Financial Stability Forum. (2009). *FSF Principles for Sound Compensation Practices.* Retrieved December 2013, from: http://www.financialstabilityboard.org/publications/r_0904b.pdf.

Financial Stability Oversight Council. (2012). *Proposed Recommendations regarding Money Market Mutual Fund Reform.* Retrieved December

2013, from: http://www.treasury.gov/initiatives/fsoc/Documents/Proposed%20Recommendations%20Regarding%20Money%20Market%20Mutual%20Fund%20Reform%20-%20November%20 13,%202012.pdf.

———. (n.d.). *Annual Report 2012.* Retrieved December 2013, from: http://www.treasury.gov/initiatives/fsoc/Documents/2012%20Potential%20 Emerging%20Threats.pdf.

———. (2013a). *Basis of the Financial Stability Oversight Council's Final Determination Regarding General Electric Capital Corporation, Inc.* Retrieved December 2013, from: http://www.treasury.gov/initiatives/fsoc/designations/Documents/Basis%20of%20Final%20 Determination%20Regarding%20General%20Electric%20Capital%20 Corporation,%20Inc.pdf.

———. (2013b). *Annual Report 2013.* Retrieved December 2013, from: http://www.treasury.gov/initiatives/fsoc/Documents/FSOC%20 2013%20Annual%20Report.pdf.

G-20. (2009). *Declaration on Strengthening the Financial System.* Retrieved December 2013, from: http://www.g20.utoronto.ca/2009/2009ifi. html.

Goodhart, C. (2010). How Should We Regulate Bank Capital and Financial Products? What Role for "Living Wills"? In A. Turner et al., *The Future of Finance: The LSE Report* (pp. 165–186). London School of Economics and Political Science. Retrieved December 2013, from: http://harr123et. files.wordpress.com/2010/07/futureoffinance-chapter51.pdf.

Goodhart, C. A. (2013). From national toward global/European regulation. In M. B. Gnan (ed.), *50 Years of Money and Finance: Lessons and Challenges* (pp. 229–261). Paris: Larcier for SUERF.

Griffin, D., & Campbell, D. (2013). *U.S. Bank Legal Bills Exceed $100 Billion.* Retrieved December 2013, from Bloomberg News: http://www. bloomberg.com/news/2013-08-28/u-s-bank-legal-bills-exceed-100-billion.html.

Gros, D. (2013). *EZ Banking Union with a Sovereign Virus.* Retrieved December 2013, from Vox Europa: http://www.voxeu.org/article/ ez-banking-union-sovereign-virus.

Haldane, A. G. (2010). *The $100 Billion Question.* Retrieved December 2013, from: http://www.bankofengland.co.uk/publications/Documents/ speeches/2010/speech433.pdf.

HMT 2012. United Kingdom Her Majesty's Treasury. *Sound Banking: Delivering Reform.* Retrieved December 2013, from: https://www.gov.uk/ government/uploads/system/uploads/attachment_data/file/211866/ icb_banking_reform_bill.pdf.

HMT 2013. United Kingdom. HM Treasury Chancellor of the Exchequer. *FPC Leverage Review. Letter from George Osborne, Chancellor to Mark Carney,*

Governor, Bank of England. Retrieved December 2013, from: http://www.bankofengland.co.uk/publications/Documents/news/2013/chancellorletter261113.pdf.

HMT/BIS 2013. United Kingdom. Her Majesty's Treasury and Department for Business, Innovation & Skills. *Banking Reform: A New Structure for Stability and Growth.* Retrieved April 2014 from: https://www.gov.uk/government/uploads/system/uploads/attachment_data/file/228995/8545.pdf.

Huertas, T. F. (2009). "The Outlook for Banking and Banking Regulation." An Address before the ICFR Inaugural Summit, "The Regulatory Response of the G-20 to the Financial Crisis," London. Retrieved January 2014, from: http://www.fsa.gov.uk/pages/Library/Communication/Speeches/2009/0401_th.shtml.

————. (2011). *Crisis: Cause, Containment and Cure* (2nd ed.). London: Palgrave Macmillan.

————. (2012a). Resolution Requires Reform. In Patrick S. Kenadjian (ed.), *Too Big to Fail – Brauchen Wir ein Sonderinsolvenzrecht für Banken?* (pp. 63–84). Berlin: de Gruyter.

————. (2012b). *A Race to the Top?* LSE Financial Markets Group Special Paper 208: Retrieved January 2014, from: http://www.lse.ac.uk/fmg/workingPapers/specialPapers/PDF/SP208.pdf.

————. (2013a). Safe to Fail. *Journal of Financial Perspectives.* Available at: http://gfsi.ey.com/the-journal-of-financial-perspectives/volume/1/issue/3/safe-to-fail_54.

————. (2013b). Banking Union. *Bank of Spain Financial Stability Review,* 31–44. Available at: http://www.bde.es/f/webbde/GAP/Secciones/Publicaciones/InformesBoletinesRevistas/RevistaEstabilidadFinanciera/13/Mayo/Fic/ref2013242.pdf.

————. (2013c). The Case for Bail-ins. In Patrick Kenadjian (ed.), *The Bank Recovery and Resolution Directive: Europe's Solution for "Too Big to Fail"* (pp. 167–188). Berlin: de Gruyter.

————. (2014a). Financial Market Infrastructures: Their Critical Role during Recovery and Resolution. *Banking Perspective: The Quarterly Journal of the Clearing House.* 2(1), 68–75.

————. (2014b). *What's a Fund For? The Case of Resolution Funds.* Forthcoming.

_____. (2014c). *A Resolvable Bank.* LSE Financial Markets Group Special Paper 230. Retrieved April 2014, from: http://www.lse.ac.uk/fmg/workingPapers/specialPapers/PDF/SP230-final.pdf.

Huertas, T. F., & Lastra, R. (2011). Living Wills. *Banco de España Revista de Estabilidad Financiera,* November 2011, pp. 23–39.

Huertas, T. F., & Nieto, M. J. (2014). *How Much Is Enough? The Case of the Resolution Fund in Europe.* Vox Europa. Retrieved April 2014, from:

http://www.voxeu.org/article/ensuring-european-resolution-fund-large-enough.

Independent Commission on Banking. (2011). *Final Report Recommendations.* Retrieved April 2014, from: https://hmt-sanctions.s3.amazonaws.com/ICB%20final%20report/ICB%2520Final%2520Report%5B1%5D.pdf.

Institute of International Finance. (2011). *Addressing Priority Issues in Cross-Border Resolution.* Retrieved May 2013, from: http://www.iif.com/IIF-CrossBorder-May2011[1].pdf.

International Monetary Fund. (2010). *A Fair and Substanital Contribution by the Financial Sector: Final Report for the G-20.* Retrieved December 2013, from: http://www.imf.org/external/np/g20/pdf/062710b.pdf.

International Organisation of Securities Commissions. (2013). *Principles for Financial Benchmarks: Final Report.* Retrieved December 2013, from: http://www.iosco.org/library/pubdocs/pdf/IOSCOPD415.pdf.

Jackson, P. (2013). Shadow Banking and New Lending Channels: Past and Future. In M. Balling & E. Gnan (eds.), *50 years of Money and Finance: Lessons and Challenges.* (Paris: Larcier), 377–414.

Joyce, M., Tong, M., & Woods, R. (2011). The United Kingdom's Quantitative Easing Policy: Design, Operation and Impact. *Bank of England Quarterly Bulletin,* (3), 200–212.

Kodres, L. E. (2013). What Is Shadow Banking? *Finance and Development,* pp. 42–43.

Kose, M., & Portillo, R. (2013). IMF Brings Together Top Economic Thinkers to Debate Crises. *IMFSurvey Magazine: IMF Research.* 20 November 2013. Retrieved January 2014 from: http://www.imf.org/external/pubs/ft/survey/so/2013/RES112113A.htm.

Lew, J. J. (2013). *Remarks at Pew Charitable Trusts.* Retrieved April 2014, from: http://www.treasury.gov/press-center/press-releases/Pages/jl2232.aspx.

Liikanen, E. (2012a). *The Case for Structural Reforms of Banking after the Crisis.* Retrieved December 2013, from: http://www.suomenpankki.fi/en/suomen_pankki/ajankohtaista/puheet/Pages/puhe_El_hleg.aspx.

———. (2012b) High-Level Expert Group on reforming the structure of the EU banking sector. *Final Report.* Retrieved December 2013, from: http://ec.europa.eu/internal_market/bank/docs/high-level_Expert_group/report_En.pdf.

Matheson, T. (2011). *Taxing Financial Transactions: Issues and Evidence.* Retrieved Deceember 2013, from IMF Working Paper 11/54: http://www.imf.org/external/pubs/ft/wp/2011/wp1154.pdf.

Mayer-Schönberger, V., & Cukier, K. (2013). *Big Data: A Revolution That Will Transform How We Live, Work, and Think.* New York: Houghton Mifflin Harcourt.

McGrath, R. G. (2013). *The End of Competitive Advantage: How to Keep Your Strategy Moving as Fast as Your Business.* Boston: Harvard Business Review Press.

Merler, S., & Pisani-Ferry, J. (2012). *Hazardous Tango: Sovereign-Bank Interdependence and Financial Stability in the Euro Area.* Retrieved December 2013, from: http://www.bruegel.org/publications/publication-detail/ publication/725-hazardous-tango-sovereign-bank-interdependence- and-financial-stability-in-the-euro-area/.

Merton, Robert C., and Perold, A. (1993). Theory of Risk Capital in Financial Firms. *Journal of Applied Corporate Finance, 6*(3): 16–32. Reprinted in Donald H. Chew, ed., *Corporate Risk Management.* New York: Columbia Business School Publishing, 2008: pp. 131–161.

Moody's Investor Service. (2013a). *Rating Methodology: Sovereign Bond Ratings.* Retrieved January 2014, from: https://www.moodys.com/ researchdocumentcontentpage.aspx?docid=PBC_157547.

———. (2013b). *Rating Methodology: Global Banks.* Retrieved January 2014, from: https://www.moodys.com/researchdocumentcontentpage. aspx?docid=PBC_154255.

Nazareth, A. (2013). *Transition Period for Swaps Push Out Rule.* Retrieved December 2013, from The Harvard Law School Forum on Corporate Governance and Financial Regulation: http://blogs.law.harvard.edu/ corpgov/2013/01/31/transition-period-for-swaps-pushout-rule/.

Organisation for Economic Cooperation and Development. (2013). *Update Report on the Work to Support the Implementation of the G20 High-Level Principles on Financial Consumer Protection.* Retrieved December 2013, from: http://www.oecd.org/daf/fin/financial-education/ G20EffectiveApproachesFCP.pdf.

OTC Derivatives Regulators Group. (2013). *Report on Agreed Understandings to Resolving Cross-Border Conflicts, Inconsistencies, Gaps and Duplicative Requirements.* Retrieved December 2013, from: http://www.cftc.gov/ ucm/groups/public/@newsroom/documents/file/odrgreport.pdf.

Perotti, E., & Suarez, J. (2011). *A Pigovian Approach to Liquidity Regulation.* Retrieved December 2013, from: http://www.imf.org/external/np/res/ seminars/2011/arc/pdf/epjs.pdf.

Poszar, Z., Adrian, T., Ashcroft, A., & Boesky, H. (2013). *"Shadow Banking" FRBNY Economic Policy Review,* pp. 1–16. Retrieved December 2013, from: http://www.newyorkfed.org/research/epr/2013/0713adri.pdf.

Powell, J. H. (2013). *Ending "Too Big to Fail."* Retrieved April 2014, from: http://www.federalreserve.gov/newsevents/speech/powell20130304a. pdf.

PRA. (2013a). Bank of England Prudential Regulation Authority. *Capital and Leverage Ratios for Major UK Banks and Building Societies. Supervisory*

Statement SS3/13. Retrieved April 2014, from: http://www.bankofeng-land.co.uk/pra/Documents/publications/policy/2013/capitalleveragess3-13.pdf.

————. (2013b). Bank of England Prudential Regulation Authority. *The Prudential Regulation Authority's Approach to Banking Supervision.* Retrieved April 2014, from: http://www.bankofengland.co.uk/publications/Documents/praapproach/bankingappr1304.pdf.

————. (2013c). Bank of England Prudential Regulation Authority. *Recovery Planning. Supervisory Statement SS 18/13.* Retrieved April 2014, from: http://www.bankofengland.co.uk/pra/Documents/publications/policy/2013/recoveryplanning1813.pdf.

————. (2014). Bank of England Prudential Regulation Authority. *Supervising International Banks: The Prudential Regulation Authority's Approach to Branch Suprvision.* Consulation Paper CP4/14. Retrieved April 2014, from: http://www.bankofengland.co.uk/pra/Documents/publications/policy/2014/branchsupcp4-14.pdf.

Reinhardt, C. M., and Rogoff, K. S. (2009). *This Time Is Different: Eight Centuries of Financial Folly.* Princeton: Princeton University Press.

Repullo, R., & Saurina, J. (2011, March). *The Countercyclical Capital Buffer of Basel III: A Critical Assessment.* Retrieved December 2013, from: ftp://ftp.cemfi.es/wp/11/1102formerversion.pdf.

Roe, M. J. (2011). The Derivatives Market's Payment Priorities as Crisis Accelerator. *Stanford Law Review, 59*(3), 539–590.

Sands, P. (2013). Banking Is Heading towards Its Spotify Moment. *Financial Times* June 30. Retrieved January 2014, from: http://www.ft.com/intl/cms/s/0/e1ae654a-c791-11e2-9c52-00144feab7de.html#axzz2qZfWGmTi.

Sants, H. (2009). *Intensive Supervision: Delivering the Best Outcomes.* Retrieved December 2013, from: http://www.fsa.gov.uk/pages/Library/Communication/Speeches/2009/1109_hs.shtml.

Schlich, S., Bijlsma, M., & Mocking, R. (2014). Improving the Monitoring of the Value of Implicit Guarantees for Bank Debt. *OECD Journal: Financial Market Trends 106.* Retrieved April 2014, from: http://www.oecd.org/daf/fin/financial-markets/Improving_monitoring_guarantees_bank_debt.pdf.

Shearman and Sterling. (2014). *Volcker Unbound.* Retrieved April 2014, from: http://www.shearman.com/en/newsinsights/publications/2014/01/volcker-unbound.

Singh, M., & Aitken, J. (2010). *The (Sizable) Role of Rehypothecation in the Shadow Banking System.* Retrieved December 2013, from IMF Working Papers 172: http://www.imf.org/external/pubs/ft/wp/2010/wp10172.pdf.

Strongin, S. H. (2013) *"Does Being More Resolvable Make a Firm More Resilient? – It Depends!"* Presentation at Federal Reserve Bank of Richmond Conference on Resolution, Washington, D.C. 18 October 2013 available at: https://www.richmondfed.org/conferences_and_Events/banking/2013/pdf/resolution_conf_panel_5_strongin_does-beingmoreresolvable.pdf.

Switzerland. Financial Market Supervisory Authority (FINMA). (2012). *Ordinance of the Swiss Financial Market Supervisory Authority on the Insolvency of Banks and Securities Dealers (Banking Insolvency Ordinance, BIO-FINMA).* Retrieved January 2014, from: http://www.admin.ch/ch/e/rs/9/952.05.en.pdf.

———. (2013). *Resolution of Global Systemically Important Banks: FINMA Position Paper on Resolution of G-SIBs.* Retrieved January 2014, from: http://www.finma.ch/e/finma/publikationen/Documents/pos-sanierung-abwicklung-20130807-e.pdf.

Tarashev, N., Borio, C., & Tsatsaronis, K. (2009). The Systemic Importance of Financial Institutions. *BIS Quarterly Review*, September, 75–87.

Tarullo, D. K. (2012, November 28). *Regulation of Foreign Banking Organizations.* Retrieved December 2013, from: http://www.federalreserve.gov/newsevents/speech/tarullo20121128a.pdf.

———. (2013). *Shadow Banking and Systemic Risk Regulation.* Retrieved December 2013, from: http://www.federalreserve.gov/newsevents/speech/tarullo20131122a.pdf.

Taylor, E., & Hübner, A. (2012). *German Regulator Vetoes Key Deutsche Bank Appointment.* Retrieved January 2014, from: http://www.reuters.com/article/2012/03/16/germany-deutschebank-idUSL5E8EG19H20120316.

Tucker, P. (2012). *Resolution: A Progress Report.* Retrieved December 2013, from: http://www.bankofengland.co.uk/publications/Documents/speeches/2012/speech568.pdf.

United Kingdom. (2013). *Financial Services (Banking Reform) Act 2013.* Retrieved December 2013, from: http://www.legislation.gov.uk/ukpga/2013/33/pdfs/ukpga_20130033_En.pdf.

United States. Department of the Treasury, Office of the Comptroller of the Currency; Federal Reserve System and Federal Deposit Insurance Corporation. UST et al. (2013). *Regulatory Capital Rules: Regulatory Capital, Enhanced Supplementary Leverage Ratio Standards for Certain Bank Holding Companies and Their Subsidiary Insured Depository Institiutions.* Retrieved December 2013, from: http://www.gpo.gov/fdsys/pkg/FR-2013–08–20/pdf/2013–20143.pdf.

Valukas, A. (2010). *United States Bankruptcy Court Southern District of New York In re Lehman Brothers. Report of Anton Valukas, Examiner.*

Retrieved December 2013, from: http://jenner.com/lehman/lehman/VOLUME%201.pdf.

Wheatley, M. (2012, September). *The Wheatley Review of LIBOR: Final Report*. Retrieved December 2013, from: http://cdn.hm-treasury.gov.uk/wheatley_review_libor_finalreport_280912.pdf.

White, L. J. (1991). *The S&L Debacle: Public Policy Lessons for Bank and Thrift Regulation*. Oxford: Oxford University Press.

Woodford, M. (2013, May). *Forward Guidance by Inflation-Targeting Central Banks*. Paper prepared for the Sveriges Riksbank conference: Two Decades of Inflation Targeting: Main Lessons and Remaining Challenges, June 2013. Retrieved December 2013, from: http://www.columbia.edu/~mw2230/RiksbankIT.pdf.

Index

Additional Tier 1 and Tier 2
capital, 29, 95–7, 113
analytics and technology, 170
anti-money laundering, 74–5
asset efficiency, 163–5
under activity approach, 163
business promotion with
clients, 163–4
and transfer pricing regime,
164–5
asset managers, 70, 144, 149
asset quality review (AQR), 56, 64

bail-in implementation, 91, 112,
135
as bankruptcy procedures,
96–8
bank with foreign branches,
118, 120
of capital instruments, 95
CET1 capital requirements, 96
conditions for, 93
and creditor hierarchy, 95
of investor instruments, 96, 98
statutory authority for, 94
via stay on investor capital, 97
balance sheet, 115
bank debt, 26
investor's risk in, 17
PD and LGD, 133
and repo market, 69
bank efficiency, 162
with respect to cost, 165–6
in use of assets, 163–4
bank failure, 40, 44, 120, see also
bank-in-resolution
causes of, 29

cost of, 1, 3, 82, 135, 173, 175
and financial crisis, 4, 11
and FMIs, 70–71
banking
activity-based view of, 144
disaggregation and technology,
142, 144, 151
structure, resolvable, 114
Banking Recovery and Resolution
Directive (BRRD), 84
bank-in-resolution
and authorities,
communication between, 105
derivative contracts, 111
investment requirement,
114–15
liquidity provision in, 88,
131–32
under margining agreements,
111
bank-in-resolution, restructuring
of
liquidation of assets, 106
need for, 105–6
rights of creditors during,
106–9
bank-in-resolution, stabilisation
of, 91, 105
access to FMIs, 103
authorisation, 102–3
bank with foreign branches, 118
effective communication,
103–5
liquidity provision for, 98–102
obstacles for, 92
recapitalisation of failed bank,
92–8

bank levies, 48
Bank of England's Prudential
    Regulatory Authority (PRA)
    on leverage requirement, 28
    as supervisor of G-SIBs, 8, 9
bank regulation, 3, 132, 173–4, *see
    also* conduct regulation and
    supervision
    aims of, 19–20
    bank levies, 48
    Basel III, *see* Basel III
    capital requirements, *see* capital
        requirements, reforming
    compliance with, 134
    derivatives market reform, *see*
        derivatives market reform
    financial transaction taxes, 47
    investment and commercial
        banking, 41–4
    liquidity regulation, *see*
        liquidity regulation
    proprietary trading,
        prohibition on, 44–5
    reforms, 5
    remuneration, 37–8
    remuneration reform, 37–8
    resolution funds, 48
    risk governance, *see* risk
        governance
    and subsidiarisation, 45–6
    taxation, 46–7
bank regulation, challenge
    associated with
    capital requirements, 138–9
    management of, *see* risk and
        return targets, sustainable
bank regulation, framework
    established by
    business practice guidelines,
        135, 136–7
    risk boundary, 134–5
banks, 175
    activity view of, 142–4
    as adviser, 145
    asset view of, 142, 144
    Basel III challenges for, 175
    becoming "safe to fail," 3, 6,
        16–17, 19
    as broker, 145
    capital conservation buffer of,
        24
    capital requirements, *see* capital
        regimes
    collateral budget, 31
    conduct regulation and
        supervision, *see* conduct
        regulation and supervision
    contractual schedule of, 30–1
    definition of, 152
    disclosure practices, 154
    execution-only role of, 150
    financial services revenue pool,
        see financial services revenue
        pool
    fostering flexibility of, 166
    future of, 1
    and governments,
        interdependence between,
        17–18
    individual capital guidance, 56
    insulated from risky trading
        activities, 39
    as intermediaries, 3, 143, 145–6
    investor obligations, *see* investor
        obligations
    leverage ratio, *see* leverage ratio
    as market-maker, 145–6
    market shares, *see* market
        shares
    in "non-traditional" activities,
        176–7
    originate to distribute strategy,
        153, 164
    pricing pressure on, 143

rating of, 18
ratings pickup, 135–6
resiliency of, 162
risk governance, *see* risk governance
as risk-transformer, 146
strategic challenge faced by, 139
structure of, 39
subsidiarisation of, 45–6
supervisory classification of, 60
targets for risk and return, 140–42
transition challenge faced by, 172
transparency, 64
banks, building key capabilities of, 166
consideration for, 167
talent development, 167–9
technology, 169–71
banks, controls for, 154
business management, 160
compliance, 161
internal audit, 161–62
risk appetite control, 155–9
risk management, 160–62
bank subsidiaries, 85, 112, 114–17, 124, 128–30, 140, 171
and parent holding company, *see* parent holding company
recapitalisation of, 131–333
reserve capital of, 131
resolution of, *see* bank with foreign branches, resolution of
write-down of parent's equity in, 116
bank supervision, 3, *see also* conduct regulation and supervision
aims of, 19–20

compliance with, 134
conduct supervision, 2
derivatives market reform, *see* derivatives market reform
investment and commercial banking, 41–4
macro-prudential, *see* macro-prudential supervision
micro-prudential, *see* micro-prudential supervision
prudential supervision, 2
reforms, 5
remuneration, 37–8
sharpening, 2
bank supervision, challenge associated with
capital requirements, 138–9
management of, *see* risk and return targets, sustainable
bank supervision, framework established by
business practice guidelines, 135, 136–7
risk boundary, 135–6
value addition, 137–8
bank with foreign branches, resolution of, 83, 117
bank with foreign branches, 117–22
hybrid approach to, 129–31
MPE approach to, 123–4, 126–7
SPE approach to, 122–6
territorial approach to, 119–21
unitary approach to, 118–19
Basel Committee on Banking Supervision
leverage ratio, *see* leverage ratio
minimum requirement of exposure, 28
risk-weighted regime tightening, 25

Basel II core Tier 1 capital, 22–3
  goodwill under, 23
  minimum equity capital
    requirement under, 24
  tangible common equity under,
    23
Basel III, 2, 38, 56, 95, 173
  accelerating adherence to,
    55–6
  Additional Tier 1 and Tier 2
    capital, 29
  alternatives to, 175–7
  challenges for banks, 175
  definition of capital, 23
  financial stability with, 173–4
  liquidity regulation, *see*
    liquidity regulation
  raised capital requirements, 22,
    24–5
  risk-weighted regime
    tightening, 25
benchmarks, manipulation of,
  71–2
bonus award determination, 37–8
borrowers' earnings, 78
bridge bank, 43, 86, 112, 120
British Banking Association, 71
business management, 160
business models, 134
  of OpCo, 171
  supervisor's review of, 52
business models, banks' review of
  intermediation and services,
    142–6
  risk analysis, 147
  "stay and/or go" decision, 147
business practice guidelines, 135,
  136–7

Canada, government debt to GDP
  of, 12
capital

definition of, 22, 26
  loss absorbency of, 29
  as tangible common equity, 21
capital conservation buffer, 24
capital flow, 6
capital markets, 11
  banks' activities in, 45, 141,
    148–9, 175
  growth in, 148
capital planning, 55–6
capital planning buffer, 56
capital raising, due diligence
  exercise for, 64, 65
capital regimes, 21, 25
capital requirements, 21
  CET1 standard, 22–3
  "gone concern," 29
capital requirements, reforming,
  22
  Basel III, *see* Basel III
  definition of capital, 23
cash outflows and inflows, 98
  buffer of liquid assets for, 30–1
  contractual schedule of, 30–1
central banks, 131–32, 186n54
  cash deposits at, 32–3
  and CFPs, 57–8
  credit to bank-in-resolution,
    101–102
  Federal Reserve, *see* Federal
    Reserve
  monetary policy, 13–14
  role in trigger process, 90,
    187n5
central counterparties (CCPs), 9,
  11–13, 23–4, 27–9, 31–2, 38,
  40, 64, 108, 114–15
collateral, 14, 69, 113, 184n22,
  185n33
  borrower's securities as, 68–9
  liquidation of, 77, 109–11
  as liquidity facility, 99–101

liquidity to bank-in-resolution, 99–101, 174
collateral budget, 31, 57, 162
commercial banking and investment banking, separation of, 39, 41–4
commercial real estate lending, 44
Commodities Futures Trading Commission (CFTC), 63
common equity Tier 1 (CET1) capital, 23–4, 105–6, 129, 131
  for bank-in-resolution, 96, 114–15
  sin bucket, 23
  tangible common equity under, 23
  vs. core Tier 1 capital standard, 22
competition
  distortion, 16–17
  between issuers, 6
conduct regulation and supervision, 2
  authorities, 150
  importance of, 71–2
  retail markets and consumer protection, 77–8, 150
  in wholesale markets, 72–7
conduct risk, score for, 158–9
constructive certainty, 123, 128–32
consumer protection, 75–6, 150
contingency funding plan (CFP), 57, 162
core Tier 1 capital standard, 22–4
cost efficiency, 165–6
counter cyclical bank capital measures, 79
counter-cyclical buffer, 24
counter-party risk, 25, 40

counter-party valuation adjustment (CVA), 27
credit market
  distortions in, 79
  in downswing, 80–
  and economic cycle, link between, 78–9
  and loan risk, 78–9
  in upswing, 79
creditor hierarchy and bail-in implementation, 95–6
creditors, 15, 17, 98, 116, 119–21, 126
  overall rating of, 18
  as owners of bank-in-resolution, 106–7
  rights during resolution process, 89–92, 107–9
  safeguards, 85–6
credit rating agencies
  rating of bank, 18
  reform of, 74
customer instruments, bail-in of, 96
customer obligations, 95

data management, 170
debt-deflation cycle, 79
"debt overhang," 66
debt providers, 17
deferred tax assets and Basel II, 23
deposit guarantee scheme (DGS)
  resolution authority coordination with, 88
deposits, 133
derivative contracts, 110–12
derivatives, 27
  operational risk associated with, 39–40
  role in financial crisis, 39

derivatives market reform
　counterparty risk regime, 40
　risks associated with, 40–1
　Swaps Push Out rule, 41
developed economies, growth of,
　148
disruptive innovation, 152
Dodd-Frank Act, 41, 44
doom loop, 15
due diligence exercise, 64

economic cycle and credit, link
　between, 79–81
economy-wide supervision,
　see macro-prudential
　supervision
emergency liquidity assistance,
　58, 90, 187n7
emerging markets, financial
　services growth in, 148–9
European Central Bank (ECB)
　quantitative easing, 14
　stress test of EU banks, 183n10
　supervision of G-SIBs, 7–9
European Commission, FTT
　proposal of, 47
European Systemic Risk Board
　(ESRB), 14, 63
European Union (EU), 46
　Banking Recovery and
　　Resolution Directive, 84
　bonus limit, 38
　on MMMF business, 67
　proposal for ring fence, 43–4

failed bank, recapitalisation of,
　92–8
　bail-in implementation, *see*
　　bail-in implementation
　investor resources for, 92
Federal Deposit Insurance
　Corporation (FDIC), 62, 128,
　189n22

Federal Reserve, 63, 68, 128,
　192n6
　on FBOs' US subsidiaries, 46,
　128
　quantitative easing, 14
　supervision of G-SIBs, 7, 9
Financial Action Task Force
　(FATF), 76
financial crisis, *see also* Great
　Recession
　and bank failure, 11
　impact on global GDP, 4–5
financial deepening, 148–9
financial firms, *see also* banks;
　global systemically
　important banks (G-SIBs);
　global systemically
　important financial
　institutions
　(G-SIFIs)
　cost of capital, 20
　making "safe to fail," 6
　reorganisation and
　　restructuring of, 5
　risks assumed by, 6
financial market infrastructures
　(FMIs), 40
　bank-in-resolution access to,
　103
　failure of, 11
　G-SIBs participation in, 10
　prudential supervision of,
　70–71
　recovery plan, 70
　robustness of, 70
financial markets, 109, 111
　benchmarks, 73
　disruption to, 4, 5, 8, 11, 15,
　19, 92
　fragmentation of, 21, 39–41,
　88, 175
　G-SIBs' share of activity in,
　9–10

Financial Policy Committee
  (FPC), 28, 64
financial services revenue pool,
  145
  capital markets, 148, 150
  changes in, 150
  developed markets, 148, 150
  emerging markets, 148–9
  and profit potential, 151–52
  wholesale markets, 150
financial stability, 173–6
Financial Stability Board (FSB),
  122
  management's roles and RAF,
    36
  proposal for haircuts on
    securities, 68
  reform agenda, 63
  on re-hypothecation, 69
  standards for resolution
    regime, 84–5
Financial Stability Oversight
  Council (FSOC), 14, 63
financial system
  contributions to growth and
    development, 6
  support to, 11, 12
financial transaction taxes
  (FTT), 47
fiscal flexibility and stimulus
  packages, 11–12
"fit and proper" status, 51, 103
forbearance, 62, 65, 86, 90,
  187n6, 187n7
foreign banking organisations
  (FBOs), 128
  US operations of, 46
foreign jurisdiction
  territorial approach of, 119–21
  unitary approach of, 118–19
"forward guidance," 13
France, government debt to GDP
  of, 12

funding costs, 138–9
FX market, G-SIBs' share of
  activity in, 9

Germany, government debt to
  GDP of, 12
global custody, 151
global GDP, financial crisis
  impact on, 4–5
global systemically important
  banks (G-SIBs), 7–8, 90
  "acquire to arbitrage" strategy,
    153
  failure of, 10, 11
  government bail out of, 19
  leverage ratio for, 28–9
  participation in FMIs, 10
  resolution of, *see* bank with
    foreign branches, resolution
    of
  share of activity in financial
    markets, 9
  supervision of, 8–9
  systemic surcharge applied to,
    24
global systemically important
  financial institutions
  (G-SIFIs)
  competitive advantage to,
    16–17
  failure and financial crisis,
    4–5
  as systemic risk, 15
good governance, review of, 51
  business models, 52
  "fit and proper" executives, 51
  internal audit, 53–4
  line management, 53
  risk appetite framework, 51
  risk management and
    compliance, 53
government debt relative to GDP,
  11–12

governments and banks,
    interdependence between,
    17–18
government security, 32
Great Recession
    downturn following, 4–5
    sluggish recovery following,
        4–5, 13
Great Recession, policy measures
        for containing
    government debt, 11–13
    monetary policy, 13–14
    support for financial
        institutions, 11, 12
Greece, 15
G-SIB stabilisation, 92

hedge funds, 76
high-grade corporate bonds, 32
home country resolution
        authority, 118–19
    MPE approach of, 123
    SPE approach of, 122
    territorial approach of, 119–21
    unitary approach of, 118–21
host country resolution authority,
    121, 125, 130
hybrid approach to resolution,
    129–30

IFRS, leverage ratio under, 26–7
implied sovereign support, 135
    bank's credit rating of, 17
    and overall rating, 18, 136
individual capital guidance,
    55–6
individual firm supervision, *see*
    micro-prudential supervision
insider trading, 76
institutional investors, 150
insurance companies, prudential
    supervision of, 70

interest rates, 13
intermediate holding company
    UK requirement for, 45
    US requirement for, 46
internal audit (IA), 54,
    161–62
investment, 79, 145, 148
    CET1 capital, 114–15, 126
    and Dodd-Frank Act, 44
    in financial institutions and
        Basel II, 23
    in money market mutual funds,
        66–7
    role in growth and
        development, 6
    in securitisations, 73
    in technology, 169–71
investment banking and
        commercial banking,
        separation of, 39, 41–4
investment strategies, 150–52,
    165–6
investor and customer
        obligations, separation of,
        112–13
    parent holding company
        structure, 114–15
    structure of liabilities, 113
investor instruments, bail-in of,
    93, 96, 18
investor obligations, 86, 95, 97,
    98, 102, 107, 110, 123
investor's risk
    in bank debt, 17
    and resolution regime, 16–17
    and supervisory regimes, 137–8
Ireland, 15
Italy, government debt to GDP
    of, 12

"know your customer" (KYC),
    76–7

"know your customer's customer"
    (KYCC), 77

LCR buffer, high-quality liquid
    assets eligible for, 33
lenders' expectations, 80–82
lending platforms, *see* loan
    platforms
leverage ratio, 25
    asset estimation, 26–7
    concept of, 26
    disclosure to investors, 28
    reporting to supervisors, 28
    and risk-weighted ratio, 25–6
    and total Tier 1 capital, 26
    of UK banks, 28
    under US GAAP and IFRS,
        26–7
liability structure and bail-in, 95
LIBOR reforms, 74
LIBOR violations, 73–4
line management, 53
liquidity buffer, 31–3
liquidity provision in bank-in-
    resolution, 96–100, 129–30,
    see also liquidity regulation
    cash inflows and outflows, 98
    collateral, 99–9
    framework agreement of
        lenders, 101–102
    framework for, 99
    unencumbered assets, 100–102
liquidity regulation, 29, 57–8
    CFPs, 57
    goals of, 56
    liquidity coverage ratio, 31–3
    liquidity risk measurement,
        30–1
    net cash outflows under stress,
        31
    net stable funding ratio
        (NSFR), 33–4

loan participations, 152
loan platforms
    challenges related to
        interfacing with, 152–3
    peer-to-peer, 152
    strategic questions related to,
        152–3
    strategy for, 153
loans, 12, 42, 44, 68, 75, 131,
    143–5, 154, 164, 177
    disclosure rules, 152, 154
    long-term, 146
    risk of, 78
    and securities, separation
        between, 153
loan syndication, 9–10

macro-prudential supervision, 50,
    65, 79
    architecture of, 63
    BSA/AQR, 64
    credit expansion and
        extension, 63
    and "debt overhang," 64
    FMIs, robustness of, 69
    objectives of, 79
    prudential supervision of SIFIs,
        69–70
    rationale for, 63
    resolvability of SIFIs, 71
    shadow banking control, *see*
        shadow banking control
market discipline, 1, 17, 109, 135
market liquidity for investors, 6
market-maker
    income earned by, 146
    inventory, 146
    value for customers, 145–6
market shares
    of G-SIBs in key products, 9
    strategic question, 150–52
    technology impact on, 151

maturity transformation, 6
micro-prudential supervision, 50
micro-supervision program, 50
   capital planning, 54–6
   "fit and proper" status, 51
   good governance, 51–4
   liquidity planning, 57–8
   recovery planning, 57–8
   supervisory intervention, *see*
    supervisory intervention
monetary policy, 11, 13–14
Monetary Policy Committee
   (MPC), 64
Money market mutual funds
   (MMMFs) with fixed NAVs
   systemic risk posed by, 65–6
   US and EU authorities
    proposals for, 66
mortgage-backed securities
   (MBS)
   purchased by Federal Reserve,
    14
   residential, 32–3
   sales of, 74–5
mortgage servicing rights and
   Basel II, 23
multiple point of entry (MPE)
   approach, resolution under,
   123, 126–8
"mutually assured
   fragmentation," 121

net cash outflows
   estimation of, 30–1
   resources for, 31
net stable funding ratio (NSFR),
   33–4
netting agreements, 111
new equity, issuing
   due diligence exercise for, 64
   economic benefit of issuing,
    63–4

non-bank financial institutions
   prudential supervision of,
    69–70
non-defaulting counterparty
   (NDC), 110

off-balance sheet vehicles,
   consolidation of, 65
OpCo, 171
operating risk, 158–9
Orderly Liquidation Authority, 87
OTC derivative contracts, 40

parent company debt, 133
parent holding company
   bankruptcy of, 116–17
   hybrid approach to resolution
    of, 129–130
   SPE approach to resolution of,
    124–6
   structure, 114–15
payment systems (PS), 10
peer-to-peer lending platforms,
   152
peripheral Eurozone countries,
   15
primary loss absorbing capacity,
   115, 188n12
pro-cyclical business, reducing or
   reversing, 63–4
profit potential assessment,
   151–52
proprietary trading, prohibition
   on, 44–5
prudential regulation, 137
prudential supervision, 2
public finances, G-SIFI impact
   on, 15

qualified financial contracts
   as barrier to resolution,
    109–110

derivative contracts, 110, 111
liquidation of collateral,
109–11
repurchase agreements, 110–11
solutions to, 111–12
quantitative easing, 13–14

recovery planning, 57–8
reforming resolution, *see*
resolution reform
re-hypothecation, 69–8
remuneration reform, 37–8
repo market
haircuts on securities taken as
collateral, 67, 110–12
re-hypothecation, 68–9
systemic risk to, 70
tri-party basis, 69
working mechanism of, 68
repurchase agreements, 110–12
reserve capital, 96, 105, 114–15,
119, 126, 129–32
resolution authority, 81–7, *see also*
home country resolution
authority; host country
resolution authority
bail-in implementation, *see*
bail-in implementation
bank-in-resolution
restructuring, *see* bank-in-
resolution, restructuring of
coordination with DGS, 88
coordination with supervisory
authorities, 88–9
preparation for resolution, 87
presumptive path followed by,
123–4
stabilisation and restructuring
responsibility, 86
resolution funds, 48, 89
resolution initiation
and creditors, 90–1

timing for, 91
resolution, overcoming barriers
to
constructive certainty, 128–32
cross-border issues, 117–28
investor and customer
obligations, 112–17
qualified financial contracts,
109–11
resolution plan, 61–2
resolution process, 97
prompt initiation of, 90–1
risks posed by delaying, 90
through sale to third party,
93–4
resolution reform
aims of, 82–3
supervisory discipline with, 135
resolution regimes, 16–17, 82
advance planning for, 84
basis for resolution fund, 89
challenge associated with,
138–9
coordinated with FMIs, 103
corrective action for
non-viability, 86
financial stability maintenance,
87–8
framework, 83
FSB key attributes, 84–5
"intervention target" of, 87
judicial review of, 89
legal basis for, 84
liquidity provision, 88
prior approval requirements,
89
and resolution authority, *see*
resolution authority
resolution tools options, 86–7
stay on rights of termination,
110–12
time frame, 89

resolution statutes, 86
resolution, triggering
    central bank role in, 90
    conditions for, 89
    and forbearance, 90
resolvability, 1, 3, 20, 29, 82
    conditions for, 83
    of ring-fenced bank, 43
    and structure of liabilities,
        112–13
retail markets and consumer
    protection, 76–7
return on assets (RoA), 138–9
return on equity (RoE), 136–7,
    139–40
ring-fenced bank
    capital requirements, 43
    EU proposal for, 43–4
    resolvability of, 43
    risk of assets in, 42
risk and return targets,
        sustainable
    combination of, 141
    consistent with regulatory
        environment, 140
    RoE and shareholder value,
        141–42
risk appetite
    allocation among line
        businesses, 159
    controlling, 158
    guidelines for setting, 156, 158
    within risk capacity, 155
risk appetite framework (RAF)
    controlling, 52–3
    establishing, 35–6
risk appetite statements (RAS), 35
risk capacity
    calculation of, 155–6
    definition of, 155
    and risk appetite, buffer
        between, 156–8, 162

risk culture, 53
risk governance, 6, 34, 133–4
    ratings pickup elimination,
        135–6
    risk appetite framework, 35–6
    risk data, 36–7
    supervisory strategy for, 135–6
risk management and
    compliance, 53, 160
risk premium and firm's debt
    capacity, 17
risk-taking behaviour, 19
risk transformation, 146
risk weighted assets (RWAs)
    minimum equity capital
        requirement for, 24
    tightening, 25, 40
rump bank, 120–21

"secular stagnation," 13
secured borrowing, 68
securities and loans, separation
    between, 153
Securities Exchange Commission
    (SEC), 63
securitisation, 153–4
senior unsecured debt, 11
    as "mezzanine" layer of capital,
        11, 95
    subject to bail-in, 97–8
service subsidiary, 171
shadow banking control
    limits on large exposures, 65
    money market mutual funds,
        65–6
    off-balance sheet vehicles, 65
    repo market control, 66–9
    restrictions on banks, 65
shareholder value and return on
    equity (RoE), 141–42
short-term interest rates, 13
sin bucket, 23

single point of entry (SPE)
approach, resolution under,
87, 122–6
Single Resolution Mechanism
(SRM), 84
sovereign guaranteed obligations,
32
sovereign wealth funds, 150
Spain
government debt to GDP,
2007–2013, 12
stability and growth.
balance between, 5
stable funding ratio, 33–4
stand-alone rating, 18–19, 134,
139, 140
statutory bail-in regime, 84, 94
stock brokerage, 145
stress testing, 56, 64, 183n10
structural reforms, 3
aims of, 19
bank regulation, *see* bank
regulation
bank supervision, *see* bank
supervision
impact of, 2
structural subordination, 133
subordinated debt, 29, 38, 95–6,
105, 114–17
subsidiarisation, 45–6
supervisors
duties of, 6–7, 86
of G-SIBs, 7–8
and macro-prudential
supervision, *see* macro-
prudential supervision
and micro-prudential
supervision, *see* micro-
prudential supervision
monitoring and minding
activities, 137–8
supervisory authority, 88

supervisory intervention, 59
bank classification,
59–60
resolution plan, 61–2
risk mitigation program, 61
skilled-person reviews, 61
Swaps Push Out rule, 41
Swiss government, structural
reform of, 45–6
systemically important financial
institutions (SIFIs)
prudential supervision of,
70–1
resolvability of, 72
systemic risk identification, 14–15

tangible common equity, 23
taxation, 46–7
taxpayer bailout of banks, 16–17
technology
capital investments in, 169
data management/analytics,
170
definition of, 169
management of, 170
and OpCo, 170
technology and competition, 142
territorial approach, resolution
under, 119–21
"too big to fail" problem
competition distortion, 16–17
credit standing of banks, 18–19
impact on public finance, 15
market discipline issues, 17–18
risks associated with, 1, 14
risk-taking, 18–19
root cause of, 15
steps towards ending, 1–2,
14–15
total Tier 1 capital, 26
transfer pricing regime and asset
efficiency, 164–5

UK banks, leverage requirement
of, 28
UK Treasury banking reform
bill, 45
unitary approach, resolution
under, 118–19
United Kingdom, 38
Financial Policy Committee
(FPC), 14, 64
government debt to GDP,
2007–2013, 12
Monetary Policy Committee
(MPC), 64
quantitative easing, 13
ring-fenced bank, 42–3
support for financial
institutions, 11, 12
United States, 38, 121
Financial Stability Oversight
Council, 63
fragmentation of global
markets, 40–1
government debt to GDP,
2007–2013, 12
as home and host, 128
leverage ratio for G-SIBs, 28–9
SPE approach, 128

support for financial
institutions, 11, 12
triple-key process, 87
US banking organisation, 42, 46,
182n34
Basel III leverage ratio for,
28–9
proprietary trading activities,
44–5
resolution of, 87
US GAAP, leverage ratio under,
26–8
US savings and loan (thrift)
industry, 192n6

Volcker Rule, 44–5

wholesale markets, 150
and anti-money laundering,
76–7
and credit rating agencies,
75
and insider trading, 75
manipulation of benchmarks,
73–4
mortgage-backed securities,
74–5

Printed and bound in Great Britain by
CPI Group (UK) Ltd, Croydon, CR0 4YY